Jesus: The Greatest Life of All

Bible Companion

BASED ON THE BOOK BY

Charles R. Swindoll

Produced in association with Creative Ministries

Insight for Living

THOMAS NELSON
Since 1798

NASHVILLE   DALLAS   MEXICO CITY   RIO DE JANEIRO   BEIJING

Jesus: The Greatest Life of All
Bible Companion

© 2007 by Charles R. Swindoll, Inc.

Published in Nashville, Tennessee, by Thomas Nelson. Thomas Nelson is a trademark of Thomas Nelson, Inc.

Thomas Nelson, Inc., titles may be purchased in bulk for educational, business, fund-raising, or sales promotional use. For information, please e-mail SpecialMarkets@ThomasNelson.com.

Published in association with Yates & Yates, LLP, Attorneys and Counselors, Orange, California.

Unless otherwise identified, Scripture quotations used in this book are from the New American Standard Bible® (NASB). © 1960, 1962, 1963, 1968, 1971, 1972, 1973, 1975, 1977, 1995 by The Lockman Foundation, La Habra, California. All rights reserved. Used by permission. (www.lockman.org)

Scripture quotations marked (MSG) are from the *The Message.* © 1993, 1994, 1995, 1996, 2000, 2001, 2002 by Eugene H. Peterson. All rights reserved. Used by permission of NavPress Publishing Group.

Scripture quotations marked (NLT) are taken from *The Holy Bible, New Living Translation.* © 1996 by Tyndale House Publishers, Inc., Wheaton, IL 60189 USA. All rights reserved. Used by permission.

Jesus: The Greatest Life of All

Library of Congress Cataloging-in-Publication Data

ISBN 978-1-4185-1776-2

Printed in the United States of America

07 08 09 10 11 RRD 5 4 3 2 1

From the Bible-Teaching Ministry of Charles R. Swindoll

Charles R. Swindoll has devoted his life to the clear, practical teaching and application of God's Word and His grace. A pastor at heart, Chuck has served as senior pastor to congregations in Texas, Massachusetts, and California. He currently pastors
Stonebriar Community Church in Frisco, Texas, but Chuck's listening audience
extends far beyond a local church body. As a leading program in Christian broadcast-
ing, *Insight for Living* airs in major Christian radio markets around the world, reaching people groups in languages they can understand. Chuck's extensive writing
ministry has also served the body of Christ worldwide, and his leadership as president and now chancellor of Dallas Theological Seminary has helped prepare and
equip a new generation for ministry. Chuck and Cynthia, his partner in life and ministry, have four grown children and ten grandchildren.

Based on the original outlines, charts, and transcripts of Charles R. Swindoll's sermons,
the Bible Companion text was developed and written by Mark W. Gaither, Th.M.,
Dallas Theological Seminary.

Original sermons, outlines, charts, and transcripts:
Copyright © and ℗ 1998, 1999 by Charles R. Swindoll, Inc.

Editor in Chief: Cynthia Swindoll, President, Insight for Living
Executive Vice President: Wayne Stiles, Th.M., D.Min., Dallas Theological
    Seminary
Theological Editors: Brie Engeler, M.A., Biblical Studies, Dallas Theological
    Seminary; Derrick G. Jeter, Th.M., Dallas Theological Seminary
Content Editor: Amy L. Snedaker, B.A., English, Rhodes College
Project Supervisor, Creative Ministries: Cari Harris, B.A., Journalism, Grand
    Canyon University

OTHER BOOKS BY THE AUTHOR

Books for Adults

Active Spirituality

Bedside Blessings

Behold . . . The Man!

The Bride

Come Before Winter

Compassion: Showing We Care in a Careless World

The Darkness and the Dawn

David: A Man of Passion and Destiny

Day by Day

Dear Graduate

Dropping Your Guard

Elijah: A Man of Heroism and Humility

Encourage Me

Encouragement for Life

Esther: A Woman of Strength and Dignity

Fascinating Stories of Forgotten Lives

The Finishing Touch

Five Meaningful Minutes a Day

Flying Closer to the Flame

For Those Who Hurt

Getting Through the Tough Stuff

God's Provision

The Grace Awakening

The Grace Awakening Devotional

Great Attitudes!

Great Days with Great Lives

Growing Deep in the Christian Life

Growing Strong in the Seasons of Life

Growing Wise in Family Life

Hand Me Another Brick

Hand Me Another Brick Bible Companion

Home: Where Life Makes Up Its Mind

Hope Again

Improving Your Serve

Intimacy with the Almighty

Job: A Man of Heroic Endurance

Joseph: A Man of Integrity and Forgiveness

Killing Giants, Pulling Thorns

Laugh Again

Leadership: Influence That Inspires

Living Above the Level of Mediocrity

Living Beyond the Daily Grind, Books I and II

The Living Insights Study Bible, general editor

Living on the Ragged Edge

Living on the Ragged Edge Workbook

Make Up Your Mind

Man to Man

Marriage: From Surviving to Thriving

Marriage: From Surviving to Thriving Workbook

Moses: A Man of Selfless Dedication

The Mystery of God's Will

Parenting: From Surviving to Thriving

Parenting: From Surviving to Thriving Workbook

Paul: A Man of Grace and Grit

The Quest for Character

Recovery: When Healing Takes Time

Contents

Contents

Contents

A Letter from Chuck

In my opinion, being a pastor is the greatest calling in the world. It is filled, for the most part, with joyful and encouraging experiences. And talk about rewarding! But some experiences can be eye-opening . . . even disturbing.

In the spring of 2006, one of our church's staff members thought it would be a good idea to take a video camera down to the local mall in Frisco, Texas, and ask a simple question—"Who is Jesus?"

As the video flickered across a small projection screen, my eyes opened a little wider and I unconsciously leaned forward in my chair. My heart sank. Seemingly bright, intelligent, well-educated people stood within a few miles of at least five churches that consistently teach the Bible with integrity, and yet none of them really knew Jesus or what He had done. A few months later when the time came for me to begin writing the next biography in the *Great Lives* series, I knew I had to answer this question.

The Bible Companion you hold in your hands is designed to introduce you to the man named Jesus. It will guide you through a study of key passages in the Bible so that you can discover for yourself why He continues to affect the lives of people two millennia after His time on earth. But I must warn you; this is no mere historical study because Jesus was no mere man. The questions and exercises in this Bible Companion will facilitate your interaction with the Bible, which presents Jesus as He presented Himself to eyewitnesses so long ago—a perplexing, confrontational, gracious, natural, *and* supernatural man who can be rejected or accepted, but not dismissed.

As you begin your investigation, I challenge you to read with an open and questioning mind. Accept the possibility that what Jesus said, did, and taught was intended to create a very different world than the one you presently occupy. In fact, you might even find that the truth He brought is intended to create a very different *you*!

Is the story of Jesus nonsense or life-changing truth? As you will soon discover, the manner in which people received Jesus's words and deeds depended greatly upon how they chose to respond to Him personally. I sincerely hope that before you reach the final lesson, you will have learned who Jesus is. But more importantly, I hope *you* will have come to know Him and experience His grace in your life.

Chuck Swindoll

CHARLES R. SWINDOLL

How to Use This Bible Companion

Who is this man? Jesus's own disciples struggled to comprehend His true nature throughout much of His ministry, despite witnessing miraculous healings and hearing scores of lessons. Even when they finally recognized Him as the long-awaited Jewish Messiah, they remained perplexed.

This Bible Companion will be your guide as you examine the Bible and discover for yourself the complete truth about Jesus. Whether you choose to complete this study individually or as part of a group, a brief introduction to the overall structure of each lesson will help you get the most out of these lessons.

LESSON ORGANIZATION

THE HEART OF THE MATTER highlights the main idea of each lesson for rapid orientation. The lesson itself is then composed of two main teaching sections for insight and application.

DISCOVERING THE WAY explores the principles of Scripture through observation and interpretation of the Bible passages and drawing out practical principles for life. Parallel passages and additional questions supplement the main Scriptures for a more in-depth study.

STARTING YOUR JOURNEY focuses on application to help you put into practice the principles of the lesson in ways that fit your personality, gifts, and level of spiritual maturity.

USING THE BIBLE COMPANION

Jesus: The Greatest Life of All is designed with individual study in mind, but it may be adapted for group study. If you choose to use this Bible Companion in a group setting, please keep in mind that many of the lessons ask personal and probing questions. These questions seek to elicit answers that reveal an individual's true character and then challenge the reader to change. Therefore, the answers to some of the questions in this Bible Companion may be potentially embarrassing if they are shared in a group setting. Care, therefore, should be taken by the group leader to prepare the group for the sensitive nature of these studies, to forgo certain questions if they appear to be too personal, and to remain perceptive to the mood and dynamics of the group if questions or answers become uncomfortable.

Whether you use this Bible Companion in groups or individually, we recommend the following method:

Prayer—Begin each lesson with prayer, asking God to teach you through His Word and to open your heart to the self-discovery afforded by the questions and text of the lesson.

Scripture—Have your Bible handy. We recommend the New American Standard Bible or another literal translation, rather than a paraphrase. As you progress through each lesson, the reading icon 🔍 will prompt you to read relevant sections of Scripture and answer questions related to the topic. You will also want to look up Scripture passages noted in parentheses.

Questions—As you encounter the questions, approach them wisely and creatively. Not every question will be applicable to each person all the time. Use the questions as general guides in your thinking rather than rigid forms to complete. If there are things you just don't understand or that you want to explore further, be sure to jot down your thoughts or questions.

SPECIAL BIBLE COMPANION FEATURES

Throughout the chapters, you'll find several special features designed to add insight or depth to your study. Use these features to enhance your study and deepen your knowledge of Scripture, history, and theology.

GETTING TO THE ROOT

While our English versions of the Scriptures are reliable, studying the original languages can often bring to light nuances of the text that are sometimes missed in translation. This feature explores the meaning of the underlying Hebrew or Greek words or phrases in a particular passage, sometimes providing parallel examples to illuminate the meaning of the inspired text.

DIGGING DEEPER

Various passages in Scripture touch on deeper theological questions or confront modern worldviews and philosophies that conflict with a biblical worldview. This feature will help you gain deeper insight into specific theological issues related to the biblical text.

DOORWAY TO HISTORY

Sometimes the chronological gap that separates us from the original author and readers clouds our understanding of a passage of Scripture. This feature takes you back in time to explore the surrounding history, culture, and customs of the world in which Jesus lived.

Part 1

The Child

(Beginnings)

Lesson 1

The Identity of Deity

SELECTED SCRIPTURES

THE HEART OF THE MATTER

More than two millennia ago, an ordinary-looking Jewish man began doing some extraordinary things. He taught a form of spirituality that focused more on the heart than the external appearance of righteousness. He healed disabilities and diseases. Moreover, He did something only God can do: He forgave sins! An encounter with the remarkable Jesus of Nazareth typically prompted the question, *Who is this man?*

Two thousand years later, people are asking the same question. Who is Jesus? Is He the Son of God, a great teacher, an ordinary man, or a myth? To answer this question, we don't have to waste time sorting through various human opinions. The Bible offers a completely reliable source of information about Jesus so we can discover His identity for ourselves.

DISCOVERING THE WAY

In a "man-on-the-street" interview conducted at a large mall in a major American city, several people were asked the question, Who is Jesus to you? Most admitted having little or no knowledge at all, others offered such answers as, "A great teacher" and "A

3

brother of Mohammed." However, not one person—among the dozens of people interviewed—answered the question with any confidence.

WHO IS THIS MAN?

Things weren't much different two thousand years ago. People having firsthand experience with Jesus had difficulty coming to terms with who He was. Of course, the confusion was not helped by the fact that He was no ordinary man! Luke 5:17–21 records an event in the life of Jesus Christ that illustrates the challenge He presented.

 Read Luke 5:17–21.

If you were present at this event, what would you have found most remarkable about what occurred?

_____

_____

_____

_____

What captured the attention of the religious leaders?
(See also Luke 7:48–49.)

_____

_____

_____

C.S. Lewis explained why the religious leaders had good reason to be upset:

Now unless the speaker is God, [forgiving someone's sins] is really so preposterous as to be comic. We can all understand how a man forgives offences against himself. You tread on my toe and I forgive you, you steal my money and I forgive you. But what should we make of a man, himself unrobbed and untrodden on, who announced that he forgave you for treading on other men's toes and stealing other men's money? Asinine fatuity is the kindest description we should give of his conduct. Yet this is what Jesus did. He told people that their sins were forgiven, and never waited to consult all the other people whom their sins had undoubtedly injured. He unhesitatingly behaved as if He was the party chiefly concerned, the person chiefly offended in all offences. This makes sense only if He really was the God whose laws are broken and whose love is wounded in every sin. In the mouth of any speaker who is not God, these words would imply what I can only regard as a silliness and conceit unrivalled by any other character in history.[1]

Mark 4:35–41 describes another incident in which the disciples of Jesus discovered that He was more than merely human.

 Read Mark 4:35–41.

What extraordinary power did Jesus demonstrate?

What does this imply about His identity?

By the time of this incident in Mark's narrative, the disciples had seen Jesus do some extraordinary things. Why do you think they were so astonished by this particular event?

HE IS THE MESSIAH

After spending perhaps as long as two years with Jesus, the disciples finally began to understand that Jesus was much more than a revolutionary Jewish teacher.

 Read Matthew 16:13–17.

Who did people in Jesus's day think he was?

_____

_____

Who did Peter say Jesus was?

_____

_____

GETTING TO THE ROOT
Reminders of the Promise
The term "Christ" comes from the Greek word *chris-tos*, which means "anointed one." The equivalent term in Hebrew is *mashiach*, from which we derive "Messiah." Peter's declaration affirmed that he believed Jesus to be the long-awaited Jewish Messiah. Peter's use of "Son of God" also drew upon an image whose roots ran deep into the soil of Israel's history. During the Exodus, God referred to Israel as "My son, My firstborn," commanding Pharaoh, "Let My son go that he may serve Me" (Exodus 4:22–23). God also spoke through the Old Testament prophet, Hosea, saying, "When Israel was a youth I loved him, and out of Egypt I called My son" (Hosea 11:1). "Anointed one" and "son of

God" were also titles historically given to Israel's rightful king (2 Samuel 22:51, Psalm 2:7).

God used these affectionate titles to affirm His unique, intimate relationship with the Hebrew people. Unfortunately, the people and the kings of Israel corrupted this special father-son relationship by choosing sin over obedience. And so they looked forward to the Messiah, a pure and righteous Hebrew king from the line of David who would represent the nation before God. By His obedience, the nation would finally inherit all of God's covenant promises.

When Peter was asked, *Who is Jesus?*, he answered that He was the long-awaited Messiah, the Son of God. This was the boldest, most profound theological declaration he knew how to make. Indeed, it contained far more truth than he realized, prompting Jesus to respond, "Flesh and blood did not reveal this to you, but My Father who is in heaven" (Matthew 16:17).

Only later did the disciples of Jesus understand the complete significance of the title "Son of God." John, one of Jesus's closest followers, opened his gospel with the simple declaration, "In the beginning was the Word." Very quickly, we are able to discern that he used the philosophical term "the Word" (*ho logos* in Greek) as a name for Jesus. *Logos* means so much that not one word or even a multitude of words can fully describe it. It connotes the very mind of God, the reasoning of God, the truth of God, and the character of God. All of that is *logos*.

Read John 1:1–4. Everywhere you see the phrase "the Word" or its pronoun, substitute the name "Jesus." Who did John say that Jesus was?

Some people believe that Jesus is not God but an immensely powerful being created by God. What specific words or phrases in John's declaration rule out this possibility?

"There are times when we find it difficult to comprehend the full intent of those words, *In the beginning was the Word*," wrote author Ray Stedman, "But if we find it difficult, how much more did His own disciples! They, of all people, would be least likely to believe that He was God, for they lived with Him and saw His humanity as none of us ever has or ever will. They must have been confronted again and again with a question that puzzled and troubled them, "Who is this man? . . ."

I have often pictured them sleeping out under the stars with our Lord on a summer night by the Sea of Galilee. I can imagine Peter or John or one of the others waking in the night, rising up on an elbow, and as he looked at the Lord Jesus sleeping beside him, saying to himself, "Is it true? Can this man be the eternal God?"[2]

According to John, the disciple closest to Jesus, the eternal God "became flesh" (John 1:14), a human being. (Lesson Two of this study will examine the theological implications of eternal God becoming a man.)

HE IS THE CREATOR

Not long after the earthly ministry of Jesus concluded, a zealous Jewish leader began a campaign of persecution to stamp out this teaching. As "a Hebrew of Hebrews" (Philippians 3:5), Paul considered any human claim of deity to be blasphemy. But after his own encounter with the evidence, he accepted the claim as true.

Read Paul's declaration about Jesus in Colossians 1:16–20. What did he say was created by Jesus Christ? Can you think of anything outside the categories mentioned by Paul?

Paul never denied the statement in Genesis 1:1 that God created the universe, so what must we interpret his statements to mean?

Who is Jesus according to Colossians 2:9?

As people in His day encountered Jesus, they may not have completely come to terms with His true identity as God. But even the religious leaders who objected to His forgiveness of sins could not dismiss His ability to heal. And even those who ultimately rejected Jesus as God recognized that He was something significantly more than an ordinary man.

STARTING YOUR JOURNEY

As we encounter Jesus in the testimony of eyewitnesses who recorded what they observed, we too must make a decision. Like the men and women He confronted two thousand years ago, we must answer the question, *Who is this man?* While we don't have the opportunity to interact with Him face-to-face as did those of His day, we do have other resources.

First, *we have a Bible we can trust.* The eyewitness testimony of Jesus's life, teaching, and ministry was carefully recorded and dutifully maintained throughout the centuries. These accounts appear in the Bible as the four Gospels: Matthew, Mark, Luke, and John. If the claims of the Bible are not trustworthy, then the God it describes either does not exist or has lied to us and is therefore not a God worth following. If, on the other hand, the Bible is trustworthy, then we must heed its message about Jesus Christ and respond accordingly.

Next, *we have a life that He sustains.* We discovered in our study of Colossians 1:16–20 that "in Him all things hold together." Jesus Christ sustains all life, and He superintends the daily experience of all people whether they acknowledge His authority as God or not. Those who believe that Jesus is God have firsthand confirmation of this truth. While those who have yet to believe have the testimony of believers. That testimony is admittedly subjective, but it is nonetheless genuine. As with all things, it must be viewed through the lens of Scripture.

Finally, *we have a church that He leads.* A church is a gathering of people who believe in Jesus Christ as God and teaches from the Bible, the authentic revelation of God to the world. Colossians 1:18 states that the risen Jesus Christ is "head of the body, the church" and as such is its leader.

To those who view Jesus Christ as simply an important historical figure, a mere man of influence that died more than two millennia ago, these claims of His deity sound preposterous—if not bizarre and confusing. But, as we have seen from our study of the gospel accounts, Jesus generally had that effect on those who encountered Him firsthand. The dilemma His identity triggers is the same today as it was then. C.S. Lewis described the quandary well:

> I am trying here to prevent anyone saying the really foolish thing that people often say about Him: "I'm ready to accept Jesus as a great moral teacher, but I don't accept His claim to be God." That is the one thing we must not say. A man who was merely a man and said the sort of things Jesus said would not be a great moral teacher. He would either be a lunatic—on a level with the man who says he is a poached egg—or else

he would be the Devil of Hell. You must make your choice. Either this man was, and is, the Son of God: or else a madman or something worse. You can shut Him up for a fool, you can spit at Him and kill Him as a demon; or you can fall at His feet and call Him Lord and God. But let us not come with any patronising nonsense about His being a great human teacher. He has not left that open to us. He did not intend to.[3]

The chart on page 12 provides a visual representation of Lewis's words and shows the implications of believing Jesus to be a liar, lunatic, or Lord.

Set aside a few moments, reflect on the following question, be as honest as you dare, and record your answer below. Who is Jesus Christ?

_____

_____

_____

_____

_____

_____

Liar, Lunatic, Legend, or Lord?

The Bible says Jesus claimed to be God
John 5:15–18; 8:58; 10:30

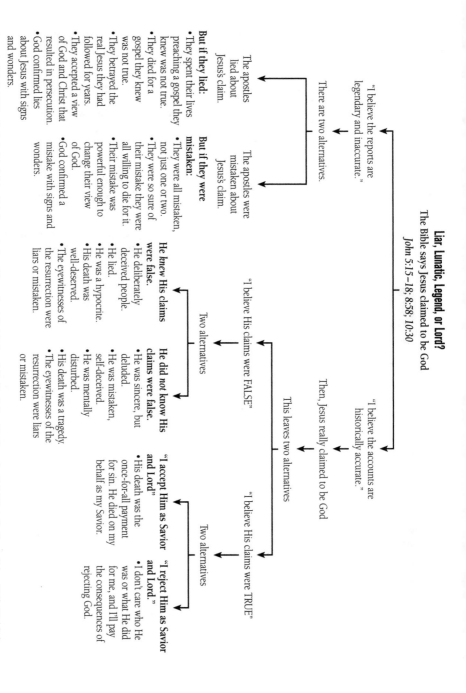

"I believe the accounts are historically accurate."

"I believe the reports are legendary and inaccurate."

Then, Jesus really claimed to be God

There are two alternatives.

This leaves two alternatives

"I believe His claims were FALSE"

"I believe His claims were TRUE"

The apostles lied about Jesus's claim.

The apostles were mistaken about Jesus's claim.

Two alternatives

Two alternatives

But if they lied:

- They spent their lives preaching a gospel they knew was not true.
- They died for a gospel they knew was not true.
- They betrayed the real Jesus they had followed for years.
- They accepted a view of God and Christ that resulted in persecution.
- God confirmed lies about Jesus with signs and wonders.

But if they were mistaken:

- They were all mistaken, not just one or two.
- They were so sure of their mistake they were all willing to die for it.
- Their mistake was powerful enough to change their view of God.
- God confirmed a mistake with signs and wonders.

He knew His claims were false.

- He deliberately deceived people.
- He lied.
- He was a hypocrite.
- His death was well-deserved.
- The eyewitnesses of the resurrection were liars or mistaken.

He did not know His claims were false.

- He was sincere, but deluded.
- He was mistaken, self-deceived.
- He was mentally disturbed.
- His death was a tragedy.
- The eyewitnesses of the resurrection were liars or mistaken.

"I accept Him as Savior and Lord."

- His death was the once-for-all payment for sin. He died on my behalf as my Savior.

"I reject Him as Savior and Lord."

- I don't care who He was or what He did for me, and I'll pay the consequences of rejecting God.

Copyright © 1981, 2006 by Charles R. Swindoll, Inc. This diagram is adapted from a chart in Josh McDowell, *The New Evidence That Demands a Verdict* (Nashville: Thomas Nelson, 1999), 158, which was based on the ideas of C. S. Lewis, *Mere Christianity*, 55–57. Material supplemented by the Creative Ministries department of Insight for Living.

12

Lesson 2

A Relationship, a Courtship . . . a Miracle

THE HEART OF THE MATTER

Let's face it; life is messy, and no one is exempt. Every life is marred by flaws, complications, inadequacies, failures, disappointments, and injustices. Mary, the mother of Jesus, never expected her life to become so complicated. Her husband, Joseph, loved her and willingly allowed her struggles to become his own. It takes grace to love someone through the difficulties in his or her life.

When God became a human being in the person of Jesus Christ, He accepted the complications and afflictions that accompany life in a world distorted by the awful effects of sin. He willingly entered the messy details of our lives. And what was His motivation? Love.

DISCOVERING THE WAY

Life was not always complicated. When God created the world and populated it with plants, animals, and the first two humans, everything ran smoothly. Then, Adam and the woman disobeyed God by eating from the tree He had declared to be "off limits." With their disobedience came awful consequences, and among the consequences was a world plunged into disorder and affliction.

13

Jesus's earthly parents, Mary and Joseph, had anything but an ordinary courtship. Both faced the pressures and complications of life in a fallen world, but they extended grace to each other as they fulfilled their unique callings.

A MESSY COURTSHIP

More than two millennia ago, a young woman named Mary lived in Nazareth, a small town in Galilee. In keeping with Jewish tradition, she was "betrothed" to a young man named Joseph. In other words, the couple's parents had arranged their marriage and sealed the agreement with a contract. During the betrothal period, typically one year, the couple continued to live with their respective families until the big day. Though they maintained their virginity, Jewish law recognized them as a married couple, and only a divorce could dissolve the contract. Furthermore, sexual immorality on the part of one gave his or her partner legal grounds for divorce and the right to exact severe punishment on the guilty party.

Read Matthew 1:18–19 and Luke 1:26–28.
Two ancient gospel writers, Matthew and Luke, recorded the events surrounding the birth of Jesus. Luke recorded the events from Mary's point of view, and Matthew recorded the events from Joseph's point of view.

What serious complication did Joseph face concerning his wife-to-be, according to Matthew 1:18?

After reading Luke 1:26–38, do you think Mary was guilty of any wrongdoing? Why, or why not?

DIGGING DEEPER

The Miracle of the Incarnation

According to John 1:14, "the Word became flesh." In other words, the Almighty, eternal Creator of the universe became a human being, an event theologians call "the incarnation." For this unprecedented event, a supernatural act was required.

In referring to Mary, both Luke and Matthew employ the Greek term *parthenos*, which means "virgin."[1] Some have argued that this term merely points to a girl who is young and eligible for marriage, not necessarily one who has not had sexual relations with a man. But the ancient Greeks took this term quite literally. For instance, the worshipers of Artemis, the goddess whose temple in Ephesus was considered one of the seven ancient wonders of the world, dogmatically claimed she was a virgin. Her virginity was a very prominent aspect of their system of belief. She was thought to protect chaste young men and women, and she symbolized the cultic power of virginity, representing "young and budding life and strict innocence."[2] Consequently, a young, unmarried woman was called a *parthenos*. In that culture, for a woman to have been anything other than a virgin before her wedding was unthinkable!

Matthew reveals that Mary was "with child by the Holy Spirit" (Matthew 1:18), meaning that God miraculously caused one of her ovum to become an embryo by supplying the required DNA without the benefit of a human father. By this supernatural method, Jesus, the God-man, entered the world just as light enters darkness (John 1:5).

According to Luke 1:56, Mary spent the three months following her encounter with the angel with her relative Elizabeth, who lived in a southern region of Israel several days' journey from Galilee. We do not know if the events describing Joseph's reaction (Matthew 1:18–25) took place before or after Mary's visit. But one thing is certain, within a week or two of returning home, her pregnancy would have become unmistakable.

How many people do you think would have believed Mary's explanation for her pregnancy? Would you have believed her? Why, or why not?

Read Matthew 1:19. What was Joseph's initial reaction?

The euphemism, "send her away secretly," could be read, *seek a quiet divorce.* In other words, Joseph planned to dissolve the marriage contract without making a public spectacle of what he assumed to be Mary's adultery. Can you imagine the thoughts that must have crossed his mind as Mary told him that she was the world's first and only pregnant virgin? In the face of being undoubtedly heartbroken, Joseph's plan reveals his gentle, graceful spirit. Fortunately, Joseph received a supernatural visit of his own in which Mary's unbelievable story was verified.

Read Matthew 1:20–21.

Joseph undoubtedly experienced mixed emotions upon hearing that Mary would be the means by which God became a man. Brainstorm a list of the emotions Joseph might have felt.

_____

_____

_____

_____

Like most people, Joseph probably wanted little more than a normal wedding, a normal marriage, and a normal life. How do you think moving forward with the wedding plans complicated his public and private life?

_____

_____

_____

_____

A COSTLY COMMITMENT

Matthew 1:22–23 states that the unusual events surrounding Jesus's birth, revealed to Joseph in his dream, took place in order to fulfill the prophecy found in Isaiah 9:6. Joseph also knew the prophecy concerning the Messiah in Micah 5:2 which revealed that He would be born in Bethlehem. This truth perplexed him because Mary and Joseph lived in Galilee. Nevertheless, despite his inability to reconcile all the events surrounding the incarnation, Joseph obeyed God.

 Read Matthew 1:24–25.

What additional sacrifice did Joseph make on his wedding day and until the baby was born?

_____

_____

_____

_____

Did the angel instruct Joseph to keep Mary a virgin?

_____

_____

Based on your reading of Matthew 1:19–25, describe Joseph's character as a husband and as a man of God.

_____

_____

_____

_____

Let's face it, life with Mary and her child was going to be messy for Joseph. The great blessing given to Mary also brought a significant amount of complications, and becoming her husband would be more than most men could bear. Nevertheless, Joseph weighed the risks, counted the cost, and willingly accepted her difficulties as his own.

STARTING YOUR JOURNEY

The story of Jesus Christ's conception and birth illustrates an important truth concerning the grace of God. Joseph could have sought a quiet divorce, found himself another nice Jewish girl, celebrated a joyous wedding, and settled into the quiet, domestic life of most men in his day. Instead, out of obedience to God, he chose to exhibit sacrificial love by entering her complicated world and sharing her burdens. What a fitting picture of the incarnation! W. Phillip Keller described it this way:

18

God's Son—God in man—would grow up fully exposed to the abrasive stresses and strains of His day. He would mature as a man amongst men. He would be One who had tasted and drunk deeply from the stream of human struggle, labor, and sweat, just to survive.

This is one of the great glories of our God. He is not a remote being detached from our desperate earth days. He is not a sublime deity who never entered the turmoil of our earth struggle. He is God, very God, who took on Himself the form of a man. He lived amongst us most of His earthly life as a carpenter's child who became a skilled craftsman in His own right. Our life was His life. Our delights were His delights. Our sorrows were His sorrows.[3]

How is your life complicated, messy, or otherwise less than ideal?

_____

_____

_____

_____

What would it mean to you for someone to sacrifice his or her own place of convenience or comfort to share in that difficulty?

_____

_____

_____

_____

The fact is . . . Jesus did exactly that!

Read each of the following passages and describe what Jesus sacrificed or endured to become one of us.

2 Corinthians 8:9 _____

Philippians 2:5–8 _____

Hebrews 2:14–15 _____

Hebrews 4:15 _____

Theologians use the word *impassible* to describe one of God's unique attributes. *Merriam-Webster's Collegiate Dictionary* defines the term as "incapable of suffering or of experiencing pain; inaccessible to injury."[4] However, in the incarnation, God willingly allowed Himself to suffer with us and on our behalf, without surrendering His essential qualities. This offers great benefits and blessings for us as believers.

> Precisely because God, especially in the Incarnation, relates Himself to the temporal-historical world and yet remains God, the Bible never represents His unchangeableness as a dead immobility, insensitive and unresponsive to what goes on in the world. The Bible never portrays an abstract God who maintains His unchangeability by remaining aloof from the world and unresponsive to what occurs in it. . . .
>
> God's unchangeability is bound up with His own reality and purpose in Christ. In Christ God has assumed an unchangeable posture toward the world: a divine, unchangeable, determined stance to be our Redeemer. From this salvific posture God will not recede nor turn aside by changing His mind. God will forever be the God whose face is Jesus Christ.[5]

This is the truth that Matthew highlighted when he quoted the Old Testament prophet: "'Behold a virgin shall be with child and shall bear a Son, and they shall call His name Immanuel,' which translated means, 'God with us'" (Matthew 1:23; see Isaiah 7:14). In the person of Jesus Christ, the Almighty, impassible God willingly entered our messy existence to share our suffering, to make our problems His own.

Think of someone whose present experience is much worse than yours and describe his or her situation.

_____

_____

_____

_____

Though it will certainly call for you to sacrifice your own personal comfort and will likely add complications to your own life, how can you help this person?

_____

_____

_____

_____

How might this resemble, even in a small way, the sacrifice Christ made for you in leaving the splendor of heaven to enter humanity's messy world?

_____

_____

_____

_____

Perhaps the best way we can genuinely appreciate the grace that Christ demonstrated by entering our mess is to willingly share in the difficulties and complications of another person's life. We can become an advocate, an encourager, a sponsor, a confidant, or even a rescuer. Not only will we bring the reality of Jesus's grace into clearer view for others, we will inevitably gain a deeper appreciation of grace ourselves.

Lesson 3

Deity in Diapers

 THE HEART OF THE MATTER

The birth of Jesus was an extraordinary event in human history; God became a man without ceasing to be the one and only God (this is called *kenosis*). While Israel's high-born, well-educated elite advanced their status and pretended to seek God's favor, their Messiah quietly slipped into the world in the unassuming hamlet of Bethlehem. Yet, for all their knowledge of prophecy and despite their anxious hope for a deliverer, few could see beyond the humble circumstances of His birth to appreciate the immense implications. Ironically, Israel's outcast and forgotten people were far more apt to recognize the truth.

 DISCOVERING THE WAY

During World War II, a chaplain decided to accompany the crew of an Army Air Force bomber on a raid over Germany. On this particular mission, they encountered heavy resistance. Enemy fighter planes swarmed the flying fortress, and antiaircraft artillery peppered the sky. In an effort to steady the men, the chaplain activated the intercom and said quietly, "It's all right, men. Have no fear. God is with you." Without hesitation, the tail gunner shouted back, "He may be with you guys up front, but He's not back here!" Within a few seconds, an enemy shell passed through the turret and out the top of the plane without detonating. After a moment of stunned silence, the tail gunner added, "Correction. God just walked in!"[1]

What an apt illustration of the first Christmas, and how well it describes the attitude of many who lived during that time! As kings and clerics postured to gain popularity with people and schemed for greater credibility with Rome, a group of shepherds—a dispossessed class of people—sat under the stars in the Judean countryside. Cast off by the decision-makers and power brokers of ancient Israel, each of whom claimed the favor of God, the shepherds probably thought, *God may be up there in Jerusalem, but He's not down here in the fields!* Then, God walked in.

THE SETTING

Two thousand years ago Israel was (as it is today) a land in turmoil, its two and a half million inhabitants bitterly divided by religious, cultural, and language barriers. An unlikely mix of Jews, Greeks, and Syrians populated the coastal towns and fertile valleys of the ancient land, and tensions among them often erupted in bloody clashes. Rome did little to discourage this volatile bitterness. As long as the people's passions were spent on each other, they weren't being vented on their conquerors.

Among these disparate groups, the Jews alone had hope for the future, for they clung to the promise that a Messiah, sent from God, would one day come to set them free. According to their Scriptures, this savior would bring swift judgment to Israel's oppressors and triumphantly reestablish the mighty throne of the great King David.[2]

Read Luke 2:1–5.

As we discovered in the previous lesson, Joseph and Mary lived in Nazareth, a small town in Galilee. Yet the prophecy of Micah (see Micah 5:2) stated that the Messiah would be born in Bethlehem, the historic birthplace of King David, which lay in Judea.

According to the passage above, what circumstance suddenly brought Joseph and Mary to Bethlehem?

_____

_____

Why was this particular town their destination?
(See also Matthew 1:1–17.)

_____

_____

Luke's statement that Joseph "went up from Galilee, from the city of Nazareth, to Judea" (Luke 2:4) may be confusing to the modern-day, "north-up" map reader. If we were looking at the map, we would say he traveled _down_ to Judea from Galilee in the north. But the ancient traveler thought in terms of elevation. Bethlehem sat on a ridge in the Judean hill country, 2,350 feet (716 meters) above sea level.

Read Luke 2:6–7.

Under what circumstances did Mary deliver her child?

_____

_____

The _International Standard Bible Encyclopedia_ describes the first-century inn this way:

> Generally speaking, inns had a bad reputation. In [the Mishnah, a collection of Jewish practical teaching], the word of an innkeeper was doubted, and [the Mishnah] places them lowest on the scale of degradation. . . . This ill repute of public inns, together with the Semitic spirit of hospitality, led the Jews and the early Christians to recommend the keeping of open house for the benefit of strangers.[3]

The registration for taxation brought hundreds, perhaps thousands of David's descendants to the little village of Bethlehem. Not only did this massive influx fill the rooms of people's homes but even the seedy inns were filled to capacity. Yet the place of Jesus's birth was even more humble than the detestable inns. For Mary gave birth in a stable and laid Jesus in a manger, a feeding trough used to hold hay for livestock.

If the wife of Caesar Augustus had delivered his heir in ancient Israel, what kind of surroundings would you expect she would enjoy? Write a short description.

What sort of reception do you think her baby would have received?

When God Became Man

It would have been unthinkable for the queen and infant prince to enjoy anything but the very best, according to the honor due them. How ironic that the Ruler of the universe should be born under such unassuming circumstances as a stable! Several years after the crucifixion, burial, and resurrection of Jesus, the apostle Paul encouraged the Christians living in Philippi to imitate the sacrifice that Christ made in setting aside the privileges of deity to become a man. Eugene Peterson's rendering in *The Message* captures the spirit of Paul's instruction.

> Think of yourselves the way Christ Jesus thought of himself. He had equal status with God but didn't think so much of himself that he had to cling to the advantages of that status no matter what. Not at all. When the time

came, he set aside the privileges of deity and took on the status of a slave, became human! Having become human, he stayed human. It was an incredibly humbling process. He didn't claim special privileges. Instead, he lived a selfless, obedient life and then died a selfless, obedient death—and the worst kind of death at that—a crucifixion. (Philippians 2:5–8 MSG)

When God became a man in the person of Jesus Christ, He did not cease to be God, nor did He lose his divine attributes, such as omnipresence and impassibility. He merely laid them aside for a time. Theologians call this choice *kenosis*, which derives from the Greek term *kenoo*, meaning "to make empty."[4]

In October of 1914, Thomas Mott Osborne entered Auburn Prison in upstate New York. Like all the other prisoners, he was photographed, fingerprinted, stripped of his possessions, issued a set of prison grays, and led to a cell, four feet wide by seven and a half feet long and seven and a half feet tall. The only difference between him and the other 1,329 inmates was the issue of freedom. On his command, he could leave the prison anytime he desired.

After his appointment to Governor Sulzer's State Commission on Prison Reform, Osborne made it his mission to live as one of the inmates, study their experience, and emerge as their advocate. He voluntarily laid aside his freedom to experience life behind bars. Although he was unlike any other inmate, he said, "I am a prisoner, locked, double locked. By no human possibility, by no act of my own, can I throw open the iron grating which shuts me from the world into this small stone vault. I am a voluntary prisoner, it is true; nevertheless even a voluntary prisoner can't unlock the door of his cell."[5]

Just as Osborne was at once free, yet confined to prison, Jesus was omnipotent (all-powerful) yet a helpless infant, dependent upon his mother's milk for survival. Born among the poorest of the poor, he set aside the privileges of deity to become the least privileged of people. That is the ultimate expression of *kenosis*. Jesus emptied all of His deity into the vessel of human flesh.

Read Luke 2:8–18.

Who received the heavenly announcement that the Messiah had been born? (*Christos* or "Christ" is the Greek equivalent of the Jewish word *mashiach*, which English renders "Messiah.") Why do you think the announcement wasn't given first to Caesar Augustus or to Herod the Great, the ruler of Judea?

_____

_____

_____

What are the implications of this?

_____

_____

_____

One respected commentary highlights the irony of the angel's announcement to shepherds. "This narrative would have challenged the values of many religious people, who despised shepherds; shepherds' work kept them from participation in the religious activities of their communities."[6]

According to verses 15–18, how did the shepherds respond to the news of their Messiah's birth?

_____

_____

 Read Matthew 2:1–12, 16.

How did the shepherds' response differ from that of Israel's rulers?

_____

_____

If you were told that your future king had just been born to a homeless mother living in a shed behind a convenience store on the outskirts of town, how would you respond?

_____

_____

_____

_____

STARTING YOUR JOURNEY

That Messiah would arrive in so humble a manner—ignored or overlooked by nearly everyone—illustrates the condition of the human heart. Those who held the reins of power or enjoyed a privileged status in Israel had little reason to seek a savior. Let's face it; wealth and power tend to insulate us from the reality of our needy condition.

The innkeeper, Herod, the politically powerful, and the social elite did not recognize the arrival of God in human form. If they had known the facts, how do you think they would have behaved?

_____

_____

As you examine your life and reflect upon your attitude toward God, do you feel you need a savior?   ☐ Yes   ☐ No

Why, or why not?

_____

_____

Is the salvation that Jesus offers—salvation from the penalty of your sin—what you hope to find in a savior? If not, what kind of savior do you desire?

_____

_____

If we allow the creature comforts of our wealthy, technologically privileged society to distract us from our true need, we will have missed the coming of Messiah as surely as the oblivious innkeeper, the status-hungry religious elite, or even the power-hungry Herod. Jesus came as one of us to save the needy—the needy in life and the needy in spirit. Only those who recognize their spiritual poverty will recognize and welcome the Savior God provided. He was deity in diapers.

Lesson 4

Responding to the Redeemer

SELECTED SCRIPTURES

THE HEART OF THE MATTER

Even as a child, Jesus had a profound effect on the people He encountered. His very presence represented a call that demanded a response, and each person responded in his or her own unique way. Shepherds rejoiced; Mary pondered; wise men worshiped; Herod revolted; and teachers marveled.

As Jesus started his public ministry, He began to issue a verbal call: "Follow Me." Those who responded found deep satisfaction. In their discipleship, they discovered the purpose for which they were made. Their experience points us to an important principle. Satisfaction in life can be found in fulfilling one's purpose, and the pursuit of that purpose begins with a positive response to the Redeemer's call.

DISCOVERING THE WAY

The birth of Jesus, though lacking in pomp and pageantry, was nevertheless a vitally important event in the lives of those who anticipated the Messiah. The birth announcement bypassed the politically powerful and social elite to include a small band of religious outcasts in Judea and an entourage of mystics from somewhere east of Israel.

RESPONSES TO HIS BIRTH

 Read Luke 2:8–20.

For whom did the angel say the "good news of great joy" was intended?

_____

_____

Look closely at 2:10–12. How many times do you see the word *you*?

_____

What does this imply?

_____

While the good news was clearly intended for all people, the shepherds received a personal invitation to see the Redeemer.

Luke 2:18–20 describes three responses to the events surrounding Jesus's birth.

How did the shepherds respond?

_____

How did "all who heard" react?

_____

In your own words, describe Mary's reaction to all that she saw and experienced.

_____

Luke used two Greek words to describe Mary's response. The first word is a compound of *with* and *keep*. It means "to keep in view" or "to preserve."[1] The second word, translated "ponder" in many Bible versions, means "to bring or throw together," "to conclude or reckon."[2] His description pictures a person gathering scattered puzzle pieces, sorting through them, and putting them together.

Read Matthew 2:1–12.

Far to the east, perhaps in Babylon, a group of men called "magi" responded to a call of their own (Matthew 2:1–12). Herodotus, a Greek historian writing more than four hundred years before Christ, identified *magoi* as "a caste of Medes who had a priestly function in the Persian Empire."[3] Most scholars believe them to have been astrologers in the tradition of the Chaldean royal advisors (Daniel 1:20; 2:2), who used their dark craft to see the future and discern the will of the gods. One of their most important functions was to validate the legitimacy of a new king. No one wanted to follow a king of whom the gods did not approve. So, the word of the magi carried enormous weight.

It is very likely that Daniel had a significant influence on the ancient tradition of these magi, who were the intellectual and cultural descendants of Nebuchadnezzar's astrologers. Daniel wrote his time-specific prophecies—some concerning the coming of Messiah—while serving as a top administrator in the Babylonian and Persian Empires (see Daniel 2:48). The magi who came to see Jesus were obviously conversant with Hebrew prophecy in general (Matthew 2:5–6). Only God knows how they made the connection between their astrological observations and the prophecies of Daniel to recognize the birth of Messiah. Regardless, they saw a miraculous star as their call to follow, and follow it they did.

Christmas pageants often portray the magi (usually three) as arriving shortly after the shepherds, but it is far more likely that they came a considerable time later, perhaps as long as two years. And we have no way of knowing how many wise men arrived. Tradition assumes three, one for each gift they brought to Jesus.

Why do you think the magi went to Israel's capital city instead of going straight to Bethlehem?

_____

_____

Why do you think Herod and "all Jerusalem" were troubled by the news of the Messiah's birth?

_____

_____

When the magi found Jesus in Bethlehem, how did they respond to Him?

_____

_____

Later in Matthew's account, we are told that Herod attempted to exploit the magi in order to discover the location of his rival and have Him destroyed. When that failed, he ordered the mass murder of all male children under the age of two in the region. But God warned Joseph to sojourn in Egypt until it was safe for them to return (Matthew 2:13–15).

RESPONSES TO HIS MISSION

Scripture doesn't reveal the intervening events in Jesus's life until He reached age twelve. Traditionally, at the age of thirteen, a Jewish boy was examined by the temple rabbis to see if he was ready to be declared a "son of the covenant." From this time forward, he was expected to fully observe the commandments and participate in community rituals.

On His family's journey to Jerusalem for the annual Passover feast, Jesus made a visit to the temple.

 Read Luke 2:41–52.

By the time Mary and Joseph found Jesus, how long had He been with the temple teachers? What was He doing?

_____

_____

How did the teachers respond to Jesus's theological and scriptural insight?

_____

_____

What reason did Jesus give Mary and Joseph for His being in the temple? What does this say about His awareness of His purpose on earth?

_____

_____

What was Jesus's purpose for coming to earth? (See Matthew 5:17; Luke 4:17-19; John 6:27-39; John 12:45-47; Acts 2:22-24)

_____

Luke 2:51 records Mary's response to finding Jesus in the temple, using the same word for "treasured" as in 2:19. We know that at some point, Mary was able to put all of the pieces together, but it was probably not until sometime late in Jesus's ministry or perhaps after His resurrection.

RESPONSES TO HIS CALL

Jesus continued to mature, and He gained a good reputation in His community. After His thirtieth birthday, the traditional age at which a Jewish man could instruct others, Jesus began His public ministry.

 Read Mark 1:16–20 and 2:14.

The apostle John recorded that Jesus taught from His home for a period of time, during which Andrew, Peter, John, and a number of other men began to recognize Him as the Messiah (John 1:35–49). Then one day, having had ample opportunity to observe Jesus and ponder His teachings, they heard their master call.

Write the names of the men Jesus called in Mark 1:16–20 and 2:14, and list what was each man doing when Jesus approached him.

_____

_____

_____

_____

What two-word call did Jesus issue to these men?

_____

What did each man do in response?

_____

How much time elapsed between Jesus's call and their response?

_____

We typically envision Jesus traveling around the Galilean countryside with a small band of men, healing and teaching in relative obscurity. But the fact is, Jesus gathered hundreds of disciples and gained widespread fame very soon after beginning His mission. Mark 3:13–15 describes an important event that marked a turning point in the ministry of Jesus. He gathered His followers for a special meeting and appointed twelve to bear the special title of "apostle," which means "messenger, envoy, one who is sent."[4] Jesus empowered them to join Him in fulfilling the purpose for which He came to earth.

By the time Jesus died on the cross, rose again from the dead, and ascended to heaven, all of His disciples had become very different people, especially the apostles. They made the decision to follow Jesus and they were never the same. They lived boldly, preached fearlessly, and died courageously. They found the unique purpose for which he or she was born, and each of their journeys began with an important first step. They responded to the call of Jesus: "Follow Me."

WHO IS HE?

During Jesus's time on earth, people responded to Him based on who they believed He was. Some of the responses are common in our own day.

Who	Passage	Who They Said He Was	Their Response
The Shepherds	Luke 2:8–20	The "Savior, who is Christ the Lord" (Luke 2:11, 17)	After visiting the Child who had been announced by the angels, they told everyone what they had seen.
The Wise Men (magi)	Matthew 2:1–12	The long-awaited "King of the Jews" (Matthew 2:2)	Seeing His star in the east, they traveled to worship Him.
The Pharisees	Matthew 9:34, 12:23–24	Called him "teacher" or "rabbi" but also accused Him of demon possession (See Jesus' response in Matthew 12:25–26)	Skepticism, condemnation, disbelief
John the Baptizer	John 1:29, 34; Matthew 11:2–6	"The Lamb of God who takes away the sin of the world," "the Son of God"	Proclaimed Jesus' deity as the promised King who would bless and judge; later he asked Jesus to confirm His identity (Matthew 11:2–6)
Neighbors, Immediate Family	Matthew 13:54–56; Mark 3:21	A "carpenter's son" who had "lost His senses"	Skeptical that this man they had known for years suddenly claimed He was God, they tried to remove Him from the public eye.
Herod Antipas the Tetrarch	Matthew 14:1–2	Feared Jesus was John the Baptist who had come back from the dead to exact judgment and revenge for his execution	Fear, disbelief
The General Public	Matthew 16:13–14	According to the disciples' report, "some [said] John the Baptist, Elijah, but still others, Jeremiah or one of the prophets," but few grasped that He was God.	Curiosity, skepticism, some belief
Peter the Apostle	Matthew 16:16	"You are the Christ, the Son of the living God."	Devotion, belief, followed Him
Caiaphas the High Priest	Matthew 26:63–68	Interrogated Jesus about His identity; Jesus acknowledged that He was the Messiah who would reign with God and return as the judge of mankind.	In a fit of rage, Caiaphas tore his robes and charged Christ with blasphemy.

Who	Passage	Who They Said He Was	Their Response
Pilate	Matthew 27:11–26, 37; John 18:28–19:22	Concluded that Jesus had done nothing to warrant civil punishment, saying "Why? What evil has He done?" (Matthew 27:23).	After declaring himself innocent of Jesus' blood, Pilate ordered Jesus' crucifixion.

STARTING YOUR JOURNEY

Because the Lord made us, He knows better than anyone what will give us satisfaction. He made us, gave us purpose, presents us with opportunities to engage in that purpose, and invites us to partake in what will make us happy and fulfilled. But we can only partake in God's purpose for our lives when we respond to His call to follow Him.

What do you believe to be your primary purpose in life? Why were you created?

_____

_____

_____

_____

To what degree do you feel you are able to live out this purpose in your life? What specific struggles seem to hinder you?

_____

_____

_____

How do you think your life would be different if you actually did what you were created to do?

_____

_____

_____

_____

Take a few moments in silence to reflect on your relationship with God. What offer has the Lord made to you that will allow you to enter into relationship with Him (Hint: Matthew 9:9)?

_____

_____

What have you done in response?

_____

_____

What will you do next?

_____

_____

_____

If you have never responded to Christ's personal call or if you're not sure what that means, turn to the section at the end of this Bible Companion titled "How to Begin a Relationship with God." We invite you to contact us if you have made or would like counsel in making a decision to accept Christ's offer of salvation by grace through faith in Him. Call or write one of our seminary-trained pastors or counselors using the information provided.

Each of us was created with a thirst to fulfill our purpose. Many wander through life trying to discover the right vocation, the right relationship, the right possessions, the right knowledge. The list of substitutes for a relationship with the Lord is endless. But these pursuits are nothing more than futile attempts to discover personal meaning, significance, or satisfaction. But only one thing will satisfy.

Jesus of Nazareth stands on the shore of your life and He has called you by name. "Follow Me."

Part 2

The Rabbi

(Teachings)

Lesson 5

Life . . . As God Intended It

SELECTED SCRIPTURES

THE HEART OF THE MATTER

Benjamin Franklin once said, "In this world nothing can be said to be certain, except death and taxes."[1] The Lord never guaranteed us a long physical life or one free from pain, sorrow, or taxes. Furthermore, the pursuit of material abundance will most often end in either failure or disappointment. Nevertheless, Jesus said that *abundant* life is available though Him.

The abundance the Lord promises will satisfy our deepest longings, but not on our terms or by our means. We must come to Him, for there is no real life apart from Christ. And we must be willing to exchange our old life for a life crafted and directed by Him.

DISCOVERING THE WAY

If we could know the future with certainty, think of all the mistakes we could avoid. Imagine how well we could manage our time and keep priorities. What fortunes we would make! Yet for all our planning and certainty, death will nonetheless claim each one of us eventually.

LIFE IS SHORT!

 Read James 4:13–15.

In these verses, what do you think James meant when he said, "You are a vapor?"

_____

_____

Rewrite this warning as though James had written it specifically for you, knowing the details of your life and what motivates you.

Dear _____ ,

(Your name)

_____

_____

_____

_____

_____

_____

_____

Most people would consider eighty years a good and long life. Yet what is eighty years compared to eternity? Our physical life runs its course in a relatively short time and then the body dissolves, leaving the immaterial part of the person to exist in eternity. Why then are we so concerned about the quality of eighty years when the vast majority of our existence will take place after our physical life has ended?

This was the primary concern of Jesus as He taught religious leaders in the temple, the social and economic elite in their homes, and the underprivileged wherever He could find them. He explained His mission this way: "I came that they may have life, and have it abundantly" (John 10:10).

MAKING THE MOST OF LIFE

 Read John 10:1–10.

Jesus certainly intended the abundant life to be something more significant than merely an improved earthly existence. A life that simply gives us more money, more time, more power, prestige, or more things to occupy our minds would be pointless. In fact, it would be little more than multiplying our futility.

Read the following passages in which Jesus talked about the abundant life and its priorities, then summarize each lesson in a single sentence.

Matthew 6:25–34

_____

_____

Matthew 13:44–46

_____

_____

Luke 12:15–21

_____

_____

Luke 18:18–30

_____

_____

> **GETTING TO THE ROOT**
> *The Real Abundant Life*
> When Jesus said that He came to give His sheep *abundant* life, He very likely used the Aramaic word *yattir,*

which means "pre-eminent, surpassing."[2] A closely related Hebrew term, *yeter*, has essentially the same meaning in the Old Testament and, in the case of wisdom literature, can refer to "the real advantage or the true excellence in life."[3] The Septuagint (the Greek translation of the Old Testament used in Jesus's day) employs the word *perissos* to express this Hebrew and Aramaic idea. *Perissos* was generally used by the Greeks to describe an overabundance of something.[4]

These terms point to a very important concept in Jewish culture. For centuries, the Hebrew people looked forward to the time when the Messiah would claim the throne of Israel and rule over the entire world. Old Testament prophecies promised that the reign of Messiah would usher in an era of superabundance (Amos 9:13; Isaiah 65:17–25). Unfortunately, the religious teachers of Jesus's day emphasized the material aspect of these promises while ignoring the more important spiritual dimension. Any material superabundance was to be a side benefit of a faithful, intimate relationship with God.

Jesus, the long-awaited Jewish Messiah, will indeed claim the throne of Israel, rule over the entire world, and usher in an unprecedented era of economic *perissos*. But all of this will occur at His *second* coming. The purpose for His first advent was to reconcile what humankind had broken: a faithful, intimate relationship with God. It is only through this intimate and faithful relationship with God that the abundant life is found, a life that is rich and overflowing in provision, community, significance, value, and purpose.

The abundant life that Christ offers has two dimensions: physical and spiritual. While many of the joys we long for await us after our present physical life has ended, the abundant and eternal kind of life can begin now. It is available to anyone who asks (Romans 10:11–13), but it's not attainable by just any means.

Read 1 John 5:11–12. To whom must we go to receive eternal life?

Read Acts 4:12. Can we find eternal life anywhere else?

Read John 3:14–16. How does one receive eternal life?

As we discovered in the previous lesson, living an abundant life begins by heeding Jesus's call, "Follow Me." At the end of that lesson, you were challenged to respond to Him. If you have not chosen to accept God's free gift of eternal life through His Son, Jesus Christ, then the rest of this lesson will have little meaning for you.

On the other hand, if you are a believer, abundant life is yours. But are you living abundantly?

STARTING YOUR JOURNEY

Second-century church father Irenaeus wrote, "For the glory of God is a living man; and the life of man consists in beholding God."[5] The Lord didn't create men and women to dolefully trudge through drab, meaningless lives. On the contrary! Consider this:

> God wants for us
> > what we would want for ourselves
> > > if we could know what He knows.

Here are four suggestions for what abundant life can include:

1. Soaring . . . above the drag of fear, superstition, and negativism.

Very often the abundant life is stifled by traditions and attitudes that are not derived from the Bible. Carefully consider the statements below to determine if they reflect your conscious or unconscious thinking.

I frequently feel that God isn't pleased with me because of something I do or fail to do.	☐ Yes	☐ No
I see the bad things that happen to me as God's way of telling me that I need to do better.	☐ Yes	☐ No
I see the good things that happen to me as God's way of affirming my choices.	☐ Yes	☐ No
I'm afraid that if I don't discern and follow God's will—His plan for my life—I will experience more difficulty and pain.	☐ Yes	☐ No
Other people seem to have a much better spiritual life than I do.	☐ Yes	☐ No
I tend to enjoy things that are not forbidden in the Bible, yet mature, Christian people say are a hindrance to my spiritual life.	☐ Yes	☐ No
I have something in mind that I would love to pursue, but I don't because the Lord might not approve and it will end in failure.	☐ Yes	☐ No

If you answered "yes" to any of the above, you might be in need of a "grace awakening." Before accepting the gift of salvation, our sin made us enemies of God, and because we deserved His wrath, we quite naturally feared Him. However, the apostle Paul wrote, "There is now no condemnation for those who are in Christ Jesus" (Romans 8:1). Unfortunately, we have a tendency to think and behave as though we still deserve God's wrath. We tiptoe around life as though we're afraid to wake a sleeping giant who would love nothing more than to grind us into dust. Nothing could be further from the truth.

The Lord wants us to live beyond the pull of fear and superstition. He wants us to do what we love, to enjoy blessings without guilt, and to honor His creative genius by living in harmony with our own uniqueness. The Lord also wants us to approach challenges with confidence, knowing that as we step out in good faith, He will direct our paths. Of all God's creatures, those who believe in His Son have every reason think positively.

2. Ignoring . . . the advice and opinions of those who operate from a strictly human perspective.

Read the following passages concerning worldly wisdom.

> **Romans 1:20–23**
> **1 Corinthians 1:18–21**
> **1 Corinthians 2:14–16**
> **1 Corinthians 3:18–20**
> **Titus 3:3–5**

Generally speaking, what does the Lord think of popular opinion?

_____

_____

What worldly perspectives can potentially keep us from enjoying a full and free life on earth?

_____

_____

The majority of public opinion will naturally run contrary to God's thinking. And, because God is in the process of transforming our minds to think in harmony with His (Romans 12:1, 1 Corinthians 2:16), we will also find ourselves more and more at odds with the thinking of the world at large.

3. Risking . . . those things that offer the illusion of security.

Risk almost always requires that we release something in the unsure hope of gaining more. Of course, the risk required for abundant living appears unwise from our point of view. But from God's perspective, the true danger is in clutching tightly to the things we find most precious. Jim Elliot, the late missionary to the Quechua Indians of Ecuador, wrote in his journal, "He is no fool who gives what he cannot keep to gain that which he cannot lose."[6]

In what (or whom) do you tend to trust for your security?

_____

_____

What sacrifices must you make to keep your security intact so that it, him, or her continues to meet your need?

_____

_____

How does relying on it, him, or her hinder you from living an abundant life?

_____

_____

Whatever we cling to as our source of security has become our god. We must feed it, nurture it, sacrifice for it, and tend to it in order to prevent the fear that it will no longer provide the safety we believe it offers. By meeting its demands, we have become its slave.

If, on the other hand, God is our source of security, we are enslaved to nothing on earth. Not money, nor relationships, nor careers, nor social standing, nor creature comforts, nor even such necessities as health, food, and love. We can safely risk the loss of all those things because the Lord is our security and provision. He has promised to meet our needs, always and forever (Matthew 6:25–34). The abundant life frees us from mundane worries and false securities. It allows us the opportunity to follow dreams and discover what it means to be utterly safe on the rugged frontier of faith.

4. Releasing . . . control of your own life.

Releasing control can be a difficult task because we are rarely conscious of what we are attempting to manage or manipulate by ourselves on a daily basis. The need for control is almost always driven by fear, and fear always has an object. Trace fear to its root and you will likely discover something you need to release into God's hands.

What do you most fear losing? (This may or may not be the same object of security you discussed with respect to "Risking.")

_____

_____

_____

_____

Which do you fear more, that God is not able or that He is not willing to manage that for you? Explain.

_____

_____

_____

_____

What might the abundant life look like if you exchanged your independence for dependence on God? Knowing that your life is "like a vapor," is it worth holding on to your own controlling tactics?

_____

_____

_____

_____

The abundant life requires that we release control of our own lives and trust the Lord. Here is a prayer that may help you release something into God's care:

Lord, I confess that I have given great energy to managing and maintaining _____,
which has been both a positive and negative part of my life. I also confess that I fear losing it or that it will change, and I'm not sure what life would be like as a result. I have looked to this for my security, for my sense of meaning or purpose, for my hope of well-being in the future, and for validation of my worth.

I cannot simply abandon this, I cannot callously drop it and walk away; it's too important to me. Instead, I place it in Your capable hands to manage and maintain on my behalf. I yield it to Your control to do as You see fit. I acknowledge that ALL Your ways are right, and I willingly accept whatever You choose to do. I choose to relinquish my old way of life in exchange for your abundant life.

Amen.

Living life as God intended is not something the Lord demands of us, nor is it a requirement for salvation. If you believe in Jesus Christ, that is, if you trust Him as your only means of reconciliation with God the Father and your only hope of eternal life in heaven, nothing else is necessary—your eternal destiny is secure. However, you could be forfeiting the blessings of heaven that are available to you right now.

The abundant life has only one requirement: We must be willing to exchange our old life for a new life, a life crafted and directed by the Lord. The abundant life is not something we claim. It is something we receive from Jesus Christ.

Lesson 6

Resting in Christ

MATTHEW 11:28–30

THE HEART OF THE MATTER

Judging by the latest pharmaceutical statistics, our culture is stressed out, anxiety ridden, depressed, and unable to sleep.

Our pursuit of happiness has taken a heavy emotional toll that physicians cite as the source of a multitude of physical illnesses. And religion, with its endless rules and demands, only adds an extra burden to an already strained life.

Jesus offered a simple—though not simplistic—solution to the problem when He said, "Come unto Me" (Matthew 11:28). The alternative He offers is rest.

DISCOVERING THE WAY

In 2005, doctors took out their pads and wrote 326,788 prescriptions to treat patients with high cholesterol, hypertension, depression, acid reflux, and sleeplessness. In other words, half of the twenty most-prescribed medications that year were dispensed to treat the symptoms of one principal disease: an epidemic called *stress*.[1] If stress is the malady of our age, then anxiety is the emotion that marks our days.

We discovered in the previous lesson that abiding in Christ produces the fruit of godly character. The apostle Paul identified the fruit as love, joy, peace, patience, kindness, goodness, faithfulness, gentleness, and self-control (Galatians 5:22–23). But these traits are nearly impossible to develop under stress. When confronted with the pressure of having to perform coupled with the demands of daily existence, then adding to that the grief of past failures and anxiety about the future, who can enjoy peace or treat others gently? Put simply, stress is a fruit-squasher!

Jesus recognized that abiding must begin with resting. Unfortunately, many of us bring to our relationship with Christ the same baggage we bring to other relationships. Even after years of discipleship, people-pleasers fear losing His favor; over-achievers try to impress Him; worriers fret; controllers make deals; guilt-trippers sulk; and the list goes on, because the variety of hang-ups is endless. However, according to Jesus, none of them are necessary.

THE INVITATION

Read Matthew 11:28.

Note that we are not invited to join an organization, to commit to a religion, to partake in specific rituals, or to offer sacrifices. Jesus Himself offers peace with God. Just before Jesus issued this invitation, He declared, "All things have been handed over to Me by My Father; and no one knows the Son except the Father; nor does anyone know the Father except the Son, and anyone to whom the Son wills to reveal Him" (Matthew 11:27). We cannot find peace with God the Father except through Jesus Christ, His Son.

To whom is the invitation given? Does Jesus exclude anyone from the offer?

What does Jesus offer and on what condition does He offer it?

As you reflect on Jesus's invitation, what thoughts or emotions does it evoke?

_____

_____

_____

When Matthew recorded the invitation of Jesus to those who are "weary" and "heavy-laden," he used two very expressive Greek terms. The first verb is active, the second, passive, picturing the "active and passive sides of human misery."[2] The first, *kopos*, refers to "beating, weariness as though one had been beaten . . . the proper word for physical tiredness induced by work, exertion or heat."[3] This term is usually used to describe the severe exhaustion of a soldier in battle or a messenger who had run several miles. Jesus also used the term to describe the affliction of worry (Matthew 6:28).

The second word, *phortizo*, is a shipping term meaning "to load."[4] It pictures a ship or an animal heavily burdened by a great weight. A frugal merchant would maximize his profit by using a limited number of pack animals so that each was laden with as much cargo as it could bear. Jesus used this image to describe hypocritical religious leaders, who "tie up heavy burdens and lay them on men's shoulders, but they themselves are unwilling to move them with so much as a finger" (Matthew 23:4).

The Jews of first-century Israel labored under a manmade burden of religiosity, an endless list of rules that governed virtually every aspect of their lives. They were spiritually demoralized and incapable of meeting further demands. They needed relief. They needed rest.

The word translated as "rest" comes from a Greek verb meaning "to cause to cease" or "to rest from labor."[5] It is closely akin to the Hebrew verb *shabat* from which derives the word *Sabbath*. Every Friday evening at sundown, faithful Jews would put an end to work until the sun set again the following day. As God originally conceived it, the Sabbath was a weekly gift of twenty-four hours during which His people could rest from their labors, enjoy a special meal with family, and celebrate their unique relationship with Him. But it had become a burdensome list of dos and don'ts. What religiosity had perverted, Jesus promised to restore. Religion says, "Work more. Try harder. Do this. Don't do that. Give until you have no more. God isn't pleased with you yet. Push, push, push, push!" Jesus looked into the hearts of exhausted, over-burdened, anxious, stressed-out people and offered a better way.

 Read Matthew 11:29–30.

Jesus made two requests. Describe them in your own words.

<hr />

<hr />

Using a standard dictionary, look up the word *yoke* and summarize the definition.

<hr />

<hr />

 DOORWAY TO HISTORY
The "Easy" Yoke
In Matthew 11:28–30, Jesus offered an intriguing invitation: "Take My yoke upon you and learn from Me." His metaphor has an obvious connotation that He clearly intended, but it also involves much more.

A yoke is a carved, wooden beam that rests across the shoulders of a pair of beasts (usually oxen or donkeys), allowing them to pull a plow or other machinery in tandem. In the Old Testament, a yoke was a symbol of burden or servitude (Genesis 27:40; Deuteronomy 28:48; 1 Kings 12:4–14; Isaiah 9:4; 10:27; Jeremiah 27:8–12; 28:2–4; Lamentations 1:14; Ezekiel 34:27). In other areas of Scripture, a yoke may symbolize close alliance or union (Numbers 25:3–5; 2 Corinthians 6:14). And in later Jewish literature, a yoke represented the totality of moral obligations that every good Jew was to take upon his shoulders ("yoke of the Torah," "yoke of the commandments," and so on).

In the first century, Jewish rabbis used the phrase "take the yoke of" to mean "become the pupil of" a particular teacher. Unfortunately, the rabbis had become notoriously harsh and even hypocritical (Matthew 23:4).

> Because of their misinterpretation, alteration, and augmentation of God's holy law, the yoke which Israel's teachers placed upon the shoulders of the people was that of a totally unwarranted legalism. It was the system of *teaching* that stressed salvation by means of strict obedience to a host of rules and regulations. Now here in [Matthew] 11:29 Jesus places his own teaching over against that to which the people had become accustomed.[6]

Jesus clearly intended to invoke this imagery of servitude in an ironic twist. Indeed, *slavery* to Christ is the greatest *freedom* a person can experience. However, the phrase "and learn from Me" suggests He intended more. Jesus said, in effect, "Are you tired? Worn out? Burned out on religion? Come to me. Get away with me and you'll recover your life. I'll show you how to take a real rest. Walk with me and work with me—watch how I do it. Learn the unforced rhythms of grace" (Matthew 11:28–29 MSG).

What kind of master and teacher did Jesus say that He is?

_____

What do you think Jesus meant when He promised, "You will find rest for your souls"?

_____

_____

Jesus offers to allow us to exchange our burdensome life for the life of rest He offers. He described His yoke as *chrestos,* which means "excellent," "serviceable," "useful," "adapted to its purpose." [7] Very frequently, a carpenter was commissioned to custom-carve a yoke to perfectly fit a particular animal. With a *chrestos* yoke, an ox or donkey could pull a plow for many hours without chafing or blistering. Furthermore, Jesus promised that His "burden" (based on the same term as "heavy-laden" in verse 28), would be light, or easy to bear.

Jesus's "yoke" illustration conveys an invitation with three parts:

- He invites us to exchange the tiresome burden of legalism ("strict obedience to a host of rules and regulations") for a lifelong Sabbath of the soul.

- He invites us to accept Him as our teacher so that we might learn how He coped, how He managed stress, how He faced the pressures of the world with tact and grace, how He forgave, how He ministered to others, and how He remained connected to the Father.

- He invites us to reject slavery to religiosity, wealth, status, relationships, or anything else that burdens us so that we might become a "slave" to Him.

The best word to describe servitude to Jesus Christ is *refreshment.*

 STARTING YOUR JOURNEY
As we have seen in the previous lessons, whatever we value most—a relationship, a job, a position of authority, our bank accounts, or our families—may be quite legitimate in its own right, but we must not allow it to consume us. For instance, the religious leaders in Jesus's day devoted much of their lives to keeping every nuance of the Old Testament commandments, not because they loved God, but because they thought their good deeds would save them from punishment. Their

meticulous law-keeping also gave them an exalted standing in the Jewish community. No one would suggest that obeying the Lord is bad. However, even something good, such as righteousness, can become a source of stress and anxiety. Neither the motive nor the stress is honoring to God.

Take a few moments to reflect on the top five sources of stress or anxiety you're experiencing today. List them below.

1. _____
2. _____
3. _____
4. _____
5. _____

Instead of pursuing, sacrificing, struggling, and fretting, why not accept Jesus's invitation to rest? That doesn't mean you have to stop caring about these things. It just means allowing Him to be in complete control of them rather than yourself. Allow Him to give and take away as He sees fit, and learn to be content with what He chooses to provide. This monumental step of faith runs contrary to everything the world believes about the pursuit of success and happiness.

If you were to surrender your pursuits to God's management and find contentment in what He chooses to provide, how do you think it would affect each of the areas you listed above? Be specific.

1. _____
2. _____
3. _____
4. _____
5. _____

If you are willing to exchange your yoke for the Lord's, personalize the prayer below and make it a regular part of your morning for the next few weeks.

Lord, as I reflect on the amount of stress and anxiety in my life, I find
_____ at the root of it. I expend a great deal of
time, thought, and energy trying to _____.
The weight of this burden has worn me down and I'm tired. I'm ready
to lay aside this heavy yoke so that I may accept your light one. I want
to rest and be refreshed, just like you promised.

Take complete control of my life, Lord. Teach me Your ways and give
me only what You think is best. I know that You love me and care more
about me than anyone, so I completely trust Your judgment. Teach me
to be content with what you provide and to avoid struggling to obtain
what I think will make me happy, secure, or significant.

Everything I am is Yours. Everything I have is Yours. I now come to
You and ask for rest.

I pray this to You, Father, in the name of Your Son, Jesus Christ.

Amen.

We have before us an open invitation from the Lord to find rest by sub-
mitting to His leadership and authority. All we have to do is trade the yoke
we carry for the one He offers. The yoke of stress we bear causes heart disease, depression, sleeplessness, headaches, and upset stomachs. The yoke
Jesus offers brings refreshment.

Cease striving, surrender, enter His rest, and enjoy a lifelong, habit-
ual Sabbath of the soul.

Lesson 7

It Is Best to Rest

HEBREWS 4:1–11

THE HEART OF THE MATTER

The invitation to enter God's rest didn't begin in the New Testament. The gift of the Sabbath is rooted in the soil of Israel's history and runs all the way back to Creation. For millennia, God has called men and women to cease striving, trust Him, and surrender to His will and His way. But very few have discovered the transcendent tranquility available to them for one very perplexing reason: unbelief. They doubt that the Lord is who He says He is and that He is in control.

DISCOVERING THE WAY

The life of a "striver" is typically characterized by dogged, relentless struggle fueled by a volatile mixture of pride, perfectionism, and self-sufficiency. And in the belly of such a life is something author Robert Wise calls the "churning place."

You discover [the churning place] in the early years of your life. It seems to be located either near the pit of your stomach or at the base of your neck, where every muscle tightens. When it begins to turn and pump like an old washing machine, you find that every other area of your life marches to its lumbering, dull, paralyzing beat.

Nothing exempts us from the relentless process created by haunting memories and bankrupt expectancies. As universal as the human heart and head, the existence of the churning place cannot be denied.

And it is not a constructive place. Positive thoughts lead to action and results, but the churning place is a tank that fills with anxieties that just settle into a stagnant infection.[1]

This does not describe the abundant life that God intends for His people. This is the *opposite*. God never asked us to meet life's pressures and demands on our own terms or by relying upon our own strength. Nor did He demand that we win His favor by assembling an impressive portfolio of good deeds. This self-reliance only produces an anxious, turbulent existence in which we become increasingly hardened and insensitive to God's voice.

Jesus said He came so that we might have life and have it abundantly (John 10:10). He said we can have that life when we abide in Him (John 15:5). And He called us to lay down the yoke of religiosity, wealth, status, relationships, or anything else that burdens us, to take up His yoke, and to learn from Him. The benefit He promised is rest (Matthew 11:28–30). Why would anyone refuse such an attractive invitation? The author of the book of Hebrews offered a straightforward explanation—one that should serve as a stern warning for us today.

A WARNING

In the verses directly preceding Hebrews 4, the author refers to an Old Testament event in which God prohibited a generation of Hebrew people from entering the Promised Land after they had wandered in the desert for years (see Numbers 14:21–23, 29).

Read Hebrews 3:16–19. Why were the people not allowed to enter the land God had promised to them?

_____

_____

THREE INITIAL OBSERVATIONS

Three initial observations will help establish the context of Hebrews 4:1–11 for our lesson.

First, the author of Hebrews linked the Old Testament story above to a New Testament truth. Bible scholar Kenneth Wuest puts it this way: "Having reminded his readers that the generation which came out of Egypt did not enter into the rest of Canaan because of unbelief, the writer now proceeds to warn them of a possible failure on their part of entering into rest in Messiah."[2]

Second, the author's primary concern is that we enter a lifelong Sabbath of the soul and claim the "rest" that Jesus offers. We do this at the moment of salvation, but we can also enjoy the benefits of a renewed relationship with Him before we get to heaven as we truly rest in His control and cease relying on ourselves.

Third, in Hebrews 4:1-11, the word *rest* is used in three distinct, yet complementary ways:

- Historically, it describes the rest God offered His covenant people, Israel.

- Theologically, it describes the rest God took on the seventh day of creation.

- Personally, it describes the rest He has made available to believers in Christ as we surrender to God's will in our lives.

 Read Hebrews 4:1–2.

On what condition should a person fear the displeasure of God?

How would you feel if you made a significant sacrifice in order to offer someone a costly gift, only to have him or her reject it?

_____

_____

How would this impact your relationship?

_____

_____

ENTERING INTO GOD'S REST

He invites us to "enter His rest," which is the metaphorical equivalent of entering a room. When we walk through a door to enter a room, we are surrounded by the space. Within that space, we are sheltered from whatever might occur outside, such as wind, rain, and the elements.

God's rest is where we are safe to lay down our fears and our anxieties. The emphasis of the Greek word translated as "rest" is on the cessation of activity. In His rest, we cease our striving and our compulsions no longer control us. Entering God's rest is a word-picture describing an intimate fellowship between the Lord and His people. So you see now, rejecting this gift of rest and peace is a very serious matter.

Read Hebrews 4:3–8.

Why didn't hearing God's promises do any good for the Israelites in the wilderness (Hebrews 4:2)?

_____

_____

How does someone enter God's rest (Hebrews 4:3)?

_____

_____

_____

When God speaks, we must do more than merely *hear* His word. We must also *believe*. This truth can be expressed in a simple formula:

HEARING + BELIEVING = RESTING

Note that the act of believing is not useful apart from the content of belief. In other words, choosing to believe in just anything is not what God desires. Believing in the wrong thing, however sincere we may be, can bring about tragic consequences.

What, specifically, are those who enter His rest supposed to believe (Hebrews 4:6)?

_____

_____

What is the danger in repetitive, persistent unbelief (Hebrews 4:7)?

_____

_____

In Genesis 1, God created the world, filled it with life, and gave everything order. He accomplished this in six days, and on the seventh day He rested, that is, He ceased from His activity. He had accomplished all that was necessary and nothing remained incomplete. To commemorate His creation and provision, He declared the seventh day a Sabbath day. But Adam and the woman chose to disobey God rather than enjoy the unending rest that began on the seventh day of creation.

Read Hebrews 4:9–11.

What more did God do after He finished creating (Genesis 2:2)?

_____

_____

_____

Once someone enters God's rest, what more must he or she do?

If something more must be done, who do you think will do it? Why?

What kinds of things do you tend to try to work out on your own? At what times do you tend to say you trust God to handle something but really still hold on tightly?

When we enter God's rest, we cease from working things out on our own. We no longer need to strive for salvation, for security, for significance, or for satisfaction. In His protected space, God provides all we need. And to enter that rest, we need only to hear and heed His Word.

STARTING YOUR JOURNEY

The world's system runs contrary to God's truth. Such ideas as grace and rest are foreign concepts here on planet Earth.

The world says, "You get what you pay for," "There ain't no such thing as a free lunch," and "God helps those who help themselves." Thoughts like these are enemies of the abundant life.

As we answer Christ's call to come to Him and we heed the command to abide, we must diligently enter His rest by choosing to keep depending on Him and surrendering to His ways. We need to give careful attention to *ceasing* and confront our rampant self-reliance. We must stop all effort to win God's favor, end our quest to earn salvation, and give up striving for what we think will give us security, significance, or satisfaction. These behaviors are rooted in unbelief.

We must also beware of three enemies of the "rest-in-faith" kind of life: presumption, panic, and pride.

Presumption is the notion that we understand exactly what we need and how to get it or that we understand the precise nature of our problems and how to solve them.

Think of a deeply felt need or a burdensome problem of yours and then complete this sentence:

If only _____, then
_____.

How much energy would you say you invest in this issue?

- ☐ **I think about this only occasionally and have never acted upon my desire.**

- ☐ **It frequently presents itself, and I often make small attempts to realize my desire.**

- ☐ **When I take an honest look at my choices in life, I see this as a recurring motive.**

- ☐ **This is on my mind most of the time, and it consistently stirs my emotions.**

- ☐ **This dominates my thoughts, and I continually try to bring about what I desire.**

- ☐ **Almost everything I do is somehow influenced by this need or problem.**

What keeps you from trusting that God's perspective is superior to your own?

_____

_____

_____

_____

What keeps you from believing that God wants you to have the best possible future?

_____

_____

_____

_____

Panic is the tendency to react to needs or difficulties impulsively. Very often we leap into action and apply a familiar fix without considering unseen issues or lasting consequences.

Unfortunately, when we panic, we often deny the Lord the opportunity to solve our problem or meet our need _His_ way. For instance, when unexpectedly faced with a significant expense, our natural reaction may be to use a credit card instead of presenting the dilemma to God first. Or we might choose to indulge a food craving instead of asking the Lord to address the emotional need that might be driving it. Or we might make a career decision based on prestige rather than how well it utilizes our gifts or supports our values.

Think of a recent crisis. What action did you take?

_____

_____

How quickly did you involve the Lord in your decision-making?

_____

_____

Pride is the feeling of self-sufficiency or adequacy to fulfill one's own need or to solve a problem without God's assistance.

Pride can hide behind things like "rugged individualism," "autonomy," "independent thinking," or even "dignity." Those can be admirable qualities in the appropriate context, but the moment they displace our dependence upon the Lord, we become guilty of pride.

How big must a need or a difficulty become before you ask for His help?

_____

_____

At what point are you willing to completely surrender all involvement in a matter to the Lord's care? (Place an 'X' on the line.)

_____

Lost my keys	Bounced a check	Wrecked my car	Lost my job	Loved one died

Read Isaiah 40:12–15; 55:8–9; Job 12:10; and Romans 11:34–36. When we will not humble ourselves before God, what are we refusing to believe?

_____

_____

These three enemies of God's rest—presumption, panic, and pride—share a common cause: unbelief. When we presume to know the right course of action, we believe we are as smart or as able as God. When we panic, we instinctively turn to our own internal resources because we doubt Him. And when we feel adequate for a task, our belief in self has diminished our view of the Almighty.

On the other hand, if we see God as He is—omnipotent, unfailingly good, and interested in us—we will not hesitate to take every matter to Him, no matter how trifling. And the degree to which we have entered

God's rest can be measured by the shrinking size of the issues we release into His capable hands.

Let's face it, strivers have a very small god. He lives in the pit of their stomachs or at the base of their necks—in the churning place. They look to this god to have their longings satisfied, their problems solved, their insecurities soothed, and their worth affirmed. With such pitiful resources, it is no wonder they strive so hard. How much easier they would rest if only they would allow the omnipotent God to carry them through life.

Won't you lay aside your unbelief and enter God's promised rest?

Lesson 8

The Astonishing Power of Jesus

THE HEART OF THE MATTER

Jesus is none other than the Almighty God in human flesh—God the Son. He shares the same divine qualities as God the Father. Any difficulty or obstacle that appears impossible from our perspective is merely an opportunity for the Lord to demonstrate His love for us. However, His limitless power remains untapped when we fail to entrust our "impossible situations" to Him.

DISCOVERING THE WAY

Our study of John 1:1–5, 14 in Lesson One revealed that Jesus has the same divine attributes as God the Father. He existed before the beginning of creation as God and then became a flesh-and-blood man. He set aside the voluntary use of His divine abilities, yet He was no less omnipotent (all-powerful) on earth than in heaven. The apostle John then described seven episodes in the life of Jesus that demonstrate the extent of His power. He has complete command over every difficulty, even over what we might consider impossible situations.

POWER OVER DEFICIENCY IN QUALITY

 Read John 2:1–10.

What problem did Mary want Jesus to solve?

_____

_____

What did Jesus do?

_____

_____

What was the headwaiter's opinion of the wine that resulted?

_____

_____

Obviously this was not a life-or-death crisis. Nevertheless, Jesus cared so much about the people involved that He decided to intervene. He was invited to solve a problem, and the solution He produced was of superior quality.

POWER OVER DISTANCE

 Read John 4:46–54.

What impossible difficulty did the royal official entrust to Jesus? How grave were the circumstances?

_____

_____

What did Jesus do in response? How much effort did He seem to exert?

_____

_____

What impact did this have on the royal official?

_____

_____

The man's hometown of Capernaum lay nearly twenty miles to the northeast of Cana, where the man first approached Jesus. This would have been at least a five-hour journey by the predominant first-century mode of transportation: feet! Nevertheless, the distance offered no challenge to Jesus's ability to heal.

POWER OVER TIME

 Read John 5:1–9.

What impossible situation did Jesus encounter at the Pool of Bethesda?

_____

_____

How long had the man been disabled?

_____

_____

What did Jesus do to bring about the man's healing?

_____

_____

Longstanding difficulties often leave us without hope for a resolution. And after experiencing it for very long—sometimes several decades—we may reconcile ourselves to the pain. But whatever the difficulty may be and however long it has existed, it is no match for the Lord's power.

POWER OVER INSUFFICIENT QUANTITY

 Read John 6:1–14.

What impossible need caused the disciples to become disheartened?

_____

_____

By what natural means could the disciples have fed the people?

_____

_____

What lesson do you think Jesus was trying to teach the disciples by involving them in this miracle?

_____

_____

How did the disciples assist Jesus in performing this miracle?

_____

_____

The lack of adequate resources frustrates nearly every human endeavor. Very rarely do we have the luxury of unlimited time and a blank check with which to accomplish something great. Fortunately, we serve a God who is never in need. As the Creator of the universe, He has complete power over the issue of quantity. He can supply any need.

POWER OVER NATURE

 Read John 6:16–21 and Mark 6:47–52.

What danger did the disciples face?

_____

What did they do to try to escape the danger?

_____

_____

How successful were they?

_____

How do these passages demonstrate that the natural elements posed no danger to Jesus?

_____

 DOORWAY TO HISTORY
Power over the Sea
To ancient people, the sea was a mysterious and dangerous place, characterized by chaos and the power to kill without warning. No fate was worse than to be swallowed by the sea and to have one's remains eaten by fish. "Both Greeks and Romans . . . recoiled with great horror at the thought of death by drowning or even burial at sea."[1] For John and other ancient writers, the sea was a symbol of evil, "a principle of disorder, violence, or unrest."[2] John's usage of the sea in his other writings, especially Revelation, designates it as the origin of cosmic evil (Revelation 12:12; 13:1; 15:2) and a symbol of creation under the curse of sin (Revelation 5:13; 7:1–3; 8:8–9; 10:2, 5–6, 8; 14:7).[3] Interestingly, the sea will no longer exist in the new creation (Revelation 21:1). [4]

Matthew and Mark also recount Jesus's astonishing power over the waves, however, John makes special use of the incident. Jesus walked across the symbol of cosmic evil that threatened to swallow the disciples, and He did so with ease while they desperately strained at the oars. While Jesus was entirely human, His power was supernatural.

In the relative comfort of our surroundings, sheltered from the impact of the elements by the marvels of modernity, it is easy to criticize the disciples for their lack of faith and understanding. After all, hadn't they heard Jesus's claim to deity and seen Him support His claim with astonishing miracles? However, we cannot afford to be smug. The dangers we face are less literal, but they are just as real. Our natural tendencies are to "strain against the oars" in an effort to save ourselves and to even fear the Lord's involvement. But He comes to us daily with the words, "It is I; do not be afraid." He has ultimate power over this world, and He offers to bring that power into our little, wave-tossed vessel.

POWER OVER MISFORTUNE

 Read John 9:1–14.

What impossible condition afflicted the man Jesus met outside the temple?

In addition to his physical affliction, what prejudice complicated his life?

How did Jesus explain the reason for the man's affliction?

As soon as Jesus finished correcting the theology of His disciples, He declared, "I am the light of the world," and then He gave the man sight. In this one act, Jesus demonstrated His authority over physical disabilities, sin, bad theology, the temple, the Sabbath, even the self-absorbed Pharisees who opposed Him. He had this opportunity because a little baby came into the world without the ability to see. God did not cause the baby's affliction; He gave it divine purpose.[5]

POWER OVER DEATH

 Read John 11:14–46.

What impossible situation did Jesus face concerning His friend Lazarus?

_____

By the time Jesus and the disciples reached Lazarus's hometown, how long had he been buried (John 11:39)?

_____

What clues in the passage reveal the pessimism of the people?

_____

_____

_____

Describe what Jesus's display of power revealed about Him.

_____

_____

Perhaps there is nothing as final in our minds as death. Even the people in the story who knew Jesus's identity as God and had seen His power in action had little hope (John 11:16, 21, 32, 37, 39).

When Adam and Eve chose to disobey God in the Garden of Eden, they introduced evil to the world, and it has twisted and spoiled everything God created. From that time forward, the world and everyone in it has suffered all kinds of affliction, including the ultimate affront to the Creator, the death of His creatures. For those who believe in Jesus Christ, however, death is not the end. Jesus made a promise, recorded for us in John 11:25–26:

> "I am the resurrection and the life; he who believes in Me will live even if he dies, and everyone who lives and believes in Me will never die."

Those who trust Jesus Christ for salvation will experience physical death but will be raised from the dead to a new kind of life, which will never end (John 11:24). Jesus then asked Martha a pivotal question: "Do you believe this?" (John 11:26) It is a question for each person to answer.

How will you answer? If you cannot answer yes, or if you are unsure, read "How to Begin a Relationship with God" at the back of this Bible Companion. If you'd like, you may call or write one of Insight for Living's seminary-trained pastors or counselors at the address listed there.

STARTING YOUR JOURNEY

The apostle John established the identity of Jesus as Almighty God and demonstrated His power using seven examples from his own eyewitness experience. Jesus exercised power over seven impossible situations involving issues of quality, distance, time, quantity, nature, misfortune, and even death. But these were only a handful of stories. Near the end of his account of Jesus's life, John testified:

> Therefore many other signs Jesus also performed in the presence of the disciples, which are not written in this book; but these have been written so that you may believe that Jesus is the Christ, the Son of God; and that believing you may have life in His name. (John 20:30–31)

If you believe, eternal life is yours. Furthermore, He promised that His power is your preservation and your protection. He didn't say that you will never suffer harm but that you will be preserved and strengthened through any difficulty and any impossible situation. He promised that every circumstance, though twisted by evil to destroy you, will become an instrument of healing in His hands (Romans 8:28).

What impossible situation do you currently face?

_____

_____

_____

_____

Briefly describe how you have tried to resolve it yourself.

_____

_____

_____

What results have you seen?

_____

_____

If you have exhausted all of your resources, run out of options, and still the difficulty you face appears to be impossible, you have a marvelous opportunity for the power of God to be manifested in your life. God invites you to bring your impossible situation to Him. If you are willing to submit your problem to the Lord, personalize the following prayer and express it to Him.

Almighty Father in Heaven,

_____ seems impossible, and I have no hope of resolving it myself, even with the help of others. However, I know that nothing is impossible for You. My greatest desire is _____, though I realize that what I want may not be what's best for everyone in the long run. So, while I want to have my way, I submit this issue to Your all-knowing, compassionate control. I trust You to do what is right, because I trust Your character.

Please give me the strength and the faith to believe you have the power to completely handle the situation. Help me to accept Your

way, even when it looks as though nothing is happening or as though things are getting worse. And help me resist the temptation to grab control of the situation back from You. If I should do something or if I should stop doing something, please give me wisdom to know what and when so that I might not frustrate Your designs.

I freely submit this to You in the name of Your Son, Jesus Christ, and by the power of Your Holy Spirit.

Amen.

Prayers such as the one above are extremely difficult to express because they put our trust in God to the test. And when we don't see Him resolving things the way we want them, we can barely stand to leave them in His care without interfering. And the Lord will rarely resolve issues according to our thinking or on our timetable. In this lesson, we have seen Jesus's power over issues of quality, distance, time, quantity, nature, misfortune, and even death. We can trust that all His ways are right and that no circumstance challenges His ability.

Lesson 9

The Ultimate Healer

 THE HEART OF THE MATTER

When Jesus, God in the flesh, ministered on earth, He exercised power over everything, including sickness and death. And He still exercises that power today, by supernaturally orchestrating natural means and occasionally—though rarely—by direct intervention. Even then, however, His direct supernatural intervention never comes through the agency of a "faith healer." Although some teach that healing can be coaxed out of God by demonstrating enough faithfulness, healing only occurs by the Lord's sovereign choice. As perplexing as this concept may be for us, it may not be His desire for every illness to be healed.

 DISCOVERING THE WAY

Tragically, the only exposure many people have to Christianity is the distorted, counterfeit religion offered by money-hungry television hucksters. Looking like a garish blend between seersucker-clad used-car salesmen and smarmy game-show hosts, they promise God's healing in exchange for donations. And they can be very convincing. These word-faith healers cleverly couch their money-making schemes in pious-sounding theology while claiming to be instruments of God's grace. In reality, however, they prey upon those made vulnerable by the pain of illness. They have perfected the fine art of balancing hope and guilt in order to convert suffering into cash.

To better understand the *true* nature of divine healing, we must understand and accept two important aspects of God's nature. First, God is all-powerful, which means He is able to do anything He chooses to do (Psalm 135:5–6; Daniel 4:35). He made the world and everything that is in it, and He can alter it at any time. Second, God is sovereign. He acts without having to consult anyone. He cannot be coerced, tricked, manipulated, or bribed into doing anything. He freely chooses to act (or not) at His own inclination, though His actions are always consistent with His unchanging, holy character.

Ancient men and women believed their pagan gods to be as capricious and depraved as humans, only more powerful. To coax blessings out of their gods, worshipers were required to bring lavish sacrifices or go to extreme lengths to demonstrate their devotion. They believed that if their gods were sufficiently impressed, their crops would grow, their enemies would fail, and their children would be healthy. The God of the Bible has always distinguished Himself as wholly distinct from the false gods of humankind's imagination. Unfortunately, today many health-wealth teachers who call themselves healers presume to treat God as ancient conjurors treated the false gods of history.

FOUR LAWS OF DIVINE HEALING

As we filter the issue of divine healing through the truth of the Bible, four timeless principles emerge from its pages. These will help us discern the truth about God, prayer, and healing.

First, *sin is both universal and personal.*

 Read Romans 5:12–14.

Who is the "one man" responsible for introducing sin into the world?

What else came into the world for the first time as a consequence of Adam's sin?

_____

How did this sin affect the rest of humankind?

_____

_____

Theologians call Adam's disobedience (Genesis 3:17–19) "original sin" because it was the first incidence of sin and all sinfulness in all people throughout all time can be traced back to his tragic choice. Each of us has inherited a diseased nature that is bent toward wrongdoing, so much so that we cannot resist the temptation to sin. In this sense, sin is universal. But when we choose to disobey, sin then becomes personal.

Second, *original sin introduced affliction, including sickness and death, into the world.*

Read Genesis 3:16–19.

What are some of the consequences of sin for women?

_____

_____

What are some of the consequences of sin for men?

_____

_____

As a result of sin, God's creation became a distorted version of what He had originally made perfect. The Lord didn't create the human body for the purpose of suffering and decay. He created the world to be a harmonious, nurturing environment for our bodies, and He created us for the purpose of intimate fellowship with Him. Now, because of sin, there's something wrong with everything, including our bodies which are susceptible to sickness and death.

Next, *sometimes sickness and death are the direct result of personal sin.*

 Read John 5:4–14 and 1 Corinthians 11:27–30.

Each of these passages clearly implies that some physical afflictions are brought on by sin. Obviously, illegal drug use destroys the body and extramarital sex can expose us to disease, but these passages of Scripture suggest that some afflictions are supernaturally allowed for the purpose of chastisement. The Lord may, as a loving act of severe mercy, allow physical affliction in order to steer a person away from destructive behavior.

And *sometimes sickness and death are not related to sin at all.*

 Read John 9:1–3.

How long had the man been blind?

_____

To what did the disciples point as the cause of his blindness?

_____

_____

When we studied this passage in the previous chapter, we noted Jesus's declaration that the man's blindness had nothing to do with *personal* sin—neither his own nor that of his parents. His physical affliction was the result of *original* sin, a consequence of sin's destructive twisting of God's creative order. However, Jesus did what God often does. He transformed sin's affliction into a divine purpose and spoke the final word in the cosmic argument between good and evil.

For a more extensive treatment of this difficult issue in children, see chapter 11, "When God's Gift Comes Specially Wrapped," in *Parenting: From Surviving to Thriving* (Charles R. Swindoll, Nashville: Word Publishing Group, 2006).

Finally, *it is not God's will that every illness be healed.*

Read Paul's perspective on illness in 2 Corinthians 12:7–10, paraphrased below:

Because of the extravagance of those revelations, and so I wouldn't get a big head, I was given the gift of a handicap to keep me in constant touch with my limitations. Satan's angel did his best to get me down; what he in fact did was push me to my knees. No danger then of walking around high and mighty! At first I didn't think of it as a gift, and begged God to remove it. Three times I did that, and then he told me,

My grace is enough; it's all you need.

My strength comes into its own in your weakness.

Once I heard that, I was glad to let it happen. I quit focusing on the handicap and began appreciating the gift. It was a case of Christ's strength moving in on my weakness. Now I take limitations in stride, and with good cheer, these limitations that cut me down to size—abuse, accidents, opposition, bad breaks. I just let Christ take over! And so the weaker I get, the stronger I become. (2 Corinthians 12:7–10 MSG)

What "gift" did Paul receive?

_____

How pleased was he to receive this gift in the beginning?

_____

_____

What did he do about it?

_____

_____

Was Paul's affliction ever healed?

_____

_____

What reason did the Lord give Paul for leaving his physical affliction unhealed?

_____

_____

By the time of Paul's death, the majority of the New Testament had poured forth from his pen as the Holy Spirit communicated divine truth through him. Furthermore, he was largely responsible for the spread of Christianity through the Western Roman Empire and for the stability of the churches there. Certainly, if anyone had enough faith and favor with God to receive divine healing, it was Paul the apostle. But that's not the way God works.

THE TRUTH ABOUT FAITH HEALERS

Faith healers typically give God all the credit for the healings that occur at their rallies, saying they are merely conduits of God's healing power. But their humility is superficial. Their words say one thing, but their theatrics and appeals for money make it very clear that in order to receive healing, one must come to them.

During the time following the resurrection of Jesus Christ and before the final piece of New Testament Scripture had been completed, God did indeed give some believers miraculous power over illness and other afflictions. However, their use of this power looked nothing like that of today's supposed healers.

 Read Acts 3:1–16.

What was the beggar's affliction, and how long had he suffered?

_____

_____

What did the apostles Peter and John do for the man?

_____

_____

How visible was the man's affliction to the community? How acute was his debilitation?

_____

_____

To what degree was the man healed and how long did the healing take?

_____

_____

What did Peter and John expect from the man before or after healing him?

_____

_____

To whom did Peter attribute the man's healing (3:6, 12, 16)?

_____

_____

How refreshing is the conduct of Peter and John, genuine agents of God's healing power! And, unlike today's faith healers, he and the other apostles were far from wealthy (Acts 3:6).

STARTING YOUR JOURNEY

While modern-day faith healers fall far short of the biblical example of healing, God does, nonetheless, heal the sick. The New Testament writer James explained how believers can respond to a person's illness.

Read James 5:14–16.

While James offered three steps for believers to follow, they are not the only ways to respond to illness, and his prescribed course of action is by no means mandatory. He merely stated that mature believers need to provide practical help for those who hurt and that prayer must not be overlooked.

Step One: Call the elders of the church.

Church leaders cannot always be aware of every physical need among those in the congregation. So, if someone has become seriously ill, the leadership must be notified.

Step Two: Elders respond by providing medical help.

The Greek language has two words that apply to the customary use of oil in the ancient world, *alepho* and *chrio*. The latter most commonly refers to the ceremonial anointing used to signify God's special blessing upon someone. For instance, the word *Christ*, which means "anointed one," comes from *chrio*. James's term, *alepho*, has more to do with the pragmatic, therapeutic use of oil, such as rubbing or massaging with it for medicinal purposes.[1] Various herbs and extracts were added to olive oil which was applied to the body to aid with a number of afflictions. In the first century, this was the best medicine available. To say that the elders were to rub the sick with oil was to say that they were to help the physically afflicted receive medical attention. Today, we would be sure to arrange a visit with a trained medical professional.

Step Three: Both submit the illness to God's will in prayer.

The process of caring for the physically afflicted must include prayer. The literal translation of James 5:15 reads, "And the prayer of faith will save the weary one." Neither medical attention nor prayer is intended to be used to the exclusion of the other. James says we are to apply both.

Again, this concept must be understood in the context of God's nature. He is all-powerful, so He can heal any illness. And He is sovereign, which means that He will act in the best interest of each person according to His unfailing goodness. While prayer is effective, we must also accept that, sooner or later, every person's physical life will come to an end. Nevertheless, for those who have accepted God's free gift of salvation through Jesus Christ, death is not the end. In a final triumph over evil, the Lord will raise us from the dead and give us eternal life in a body that cannot be harmed (1 Thessalonians 4:13–18; Philippians 3:20–21)!

FIVE PRINCIPLES REGARDING DIVINE HEALING

To keep the issue of divine healing in perspective and to help dispel the confusion that physical suffering can cause, remember these five principles.

1. The will of God is paramount. Respect it.

God's will is sometimes difficult to understand from our limited earthbound perspective. It is even more difficult to accept when it involves great suffering. Even as we pray, we must remember that God is right in all His ways, our suffering is deeply felt by Him, and for those who are His, all suffering will become the means by which He brings greater blessings later (Romans 8:26–28; 1 Peter 5:10).

2. Medical assistance is imperative. Seek it.

Prayer was never intended to replace competent medical care. God's grace to all people—not just to those who have answered His call—includes the gift of medical science. In fact, God may choose to answer your prayer for healing through the hands of an unbelieving physician (Luke 10:33–35).

3. Intercessory prayer is God's commandment. Obey it.

As we do everything within our power to bring healing to others, we do so under the providence of God. He invites us to give all matters over to Him because He cares deeply for those who hurt (Philippians 4:6). We can trust Him to do what is right (Matthew 7:7–11).

4. Confession of sins is healthy. Practice it.

Not all sickness is related to the personal sins of the one who is afflicted; however we cannot always rule it out. Confession and repentance of sins—even those we consider insignificant—are never inappropriate. Even if the sin has nothing to do with the illness, confession and repentance help keep our relationship with the Lord free of distracting issues (James 5:16; 1 John 1:8–9).

5. All healing is of God. Celebrate it.

Whenever someone's health has been restored, whether by the expertise of a medical professional or through direct, supernatural intervention, God deserves the credit. We are never mistaken to praise God and thank Him for healing and sustained health (James 1:17; 1 John 5:14–15).

God can and does heal today. We are wise to ask Him for relief from physical affliction, trusting that He will do what is right, even if we don't understand His actions. He does not need the assistance of people to provide miraculous healing. In fact, He invites us to come to Him directly. Nevertheless, we are foolish to reject His provision of healing through trained medical professionals and modern medications.

If you are seriously ill, call your physician and call for mature Christians to join you in prayer.

Lesson 10

Abiding in Christ

JOHN 15:1–11

THE HEART OF THE MATTER

No one wants to be called a good-for-nothing. But that's exactly what God calls believers who refuse to "abide in Christ." Life as God intended it should benefit not only the person who receives salvation but also the people with whom the new believer comes into contact. So, if his or her character doesn't begin to evidence the same qualities that distinguished Jesus, something has gone terribly wrong. Just as the branch of a grapevine should bear grapes, a believer should bear the fruit of a Christ-like character. However, only someone who remains in obedient relationship with Christ can bear fruit and thus fulfill his or her purpose.

DISCOVERING THE WAY

Jesus began His public ministry by calling individuals to "Follow me." As crowds began to gather around Him, He invited them: "Come to me." Then, on the eve of His arrest and the trials that would lead to His crucifixion, Jesus celebrated the traditional Passover meal with the men He had selected to continue the ministry. At one point in the evening, He commanded them, "Abide in Me." To illustrate what He meant by that unusual request, Jesus painted a word-picture using elements that would have been very familiar to His audience.

As we begin to analyze this vivid picture of the believer's life in Christ, four observations will be helpful. First, Jesus's lesson in this passage was intended for believers only. Second, He utilized a symbol that was very familiar to the people He taught, though it may not seem very vivid to us today. Third, the central point of Jesus's lesson addressed the concept of "abiding" in Him. Our temptation will be to find hidden meanings and attach special significance to elements within the word-picture that Jesus never intended. So, we will have to keep our eyes trained on the central issue as we ignore distractions. Fourth, the result of abiding is the bearing of "fruit"—Christ-like character qualities and actions—which gives meaning and purpose to the life of the believer.

THE *TRUE* VINE

 Read John 15:1–4.

What agricultural image did Jesus use? Who is the grapevine and who is the "vinedresser," the one who tends the vineyard?

_____

_____

_____

_____

What is the primary purpose of a grapevine?

_____

_____

_____

How would you describe a branch that never produced grapes but was attached to an otherwise healthy vine?

_____

_____

"Abiding in Christ" is admittedly an abstract concept that defies description. Scholars debate on what it means in practical terms. According to *Merriam-Webster's Collegiate Dictionary, abide* means "to remain stable or fixed in a state, to continue in a place."[1] For our purposes, abiding in Christ means remaining in obedient relationship with Him. That can be seen as drawing near to God, living dependently on Him, acknowledging that you can do nothing good without Him, and trusting Him with your whole heart rather than your own understanding. Jesus shared the vineyard illustration with His disciples to help them understand that grace not only initiates the relationship between God and a believer but grace also sustains it.

What are some practical ways you remain in obedient relationship with Christ?

_____

_____

_____

The vineyard metaphor would have been familiar to any Jew. It was a popular symbol of Israel in the Old Testament (Psalm 80:8–9; Ezekiel 15:1–5; Hosea 10:1), and it was often depicted as either unproductive or producing bitter grapes. Though chosen by God, Israel had always been a defective vine that frequently frustrated God, who often felt the best course of action was to plow it under (Isaiah 5:1–7). Fortunately, thanks only to His amazing grace, He didn't. Instead, He sent His Son to do what Israel could not.

Jesus began His lesson to the disciples with the bold declaration, "I am the true vine" (John 15:1). In other words, where Israel had failed, the Messiah would prove faithful.

THE VINEDRESSER

Read Isaiah 5:1–6 and John 15:2. How does God treat each of these vines?

_____

_____

_____

_____

The image in John 15:2 describes the care of a vinedresser tending to the needs of the branches so that they will produce a full harvest of high-quality grapes. Many versions of the Bible translate a key Greek term in this verse as "takes away," "removes," or even "cuts off," but its primary definition is "to lift from the ground."[2] The word can and often does mean "to lift with a view to carrying, to carry off or put away,"[3] but in keeping with the metaphor, Jesus most likely referred to the vinedresser's practice of lifting a sagging branch and tying it to the trellis—a procedure called "training." The vinedresser also carefully prunes the branches to encourage healthy growth.

BEARING FRUIT

Having established the _position_ of believers in relation to Himself, Jesus turned to the subject of the believer's _production._

Read John 15:4–6.

What is the branch's sole responsibility?

_____

_____

What is the result if someone does not abide in Christ?

_____

_____

What will occur if someone *does* abide in Him?

_____

If a branch draws no life from the vine, what can it be used for?

_____

Note that Jesus never said it was the responsibility of the branch to grow grapes. A branch cannot bear fruit on its own. However, if it maintains a strong connection to the vine so that it receives life-giving sap, grapes will soon be hanging by the bunches.

So, what does it mean for the Christian to "bear fruit?" Some have suggested that the fruit of a believer is another believer; in other words, a person has chosen to place his or her faith in Jesus Christ as a result of the believer's influence. This may be what Jesus had in mind, but "fruit" may also refer to another noteworthy product. The apostle Paul used the image of fruit to describe the character qualities that should mark a healthy, mature believer.

Read Galatians 5:22–23. List the "fruit" of the Holy Spirit's transforming work.

_____

_____

_____

As you review these examples of Christ-like qualities and reflect upon your life, how would you describe the fruit you are bearing?

☐ My branch is heavy with grapes.

☐ My fruit would make a respectable harvest.

☐ My fruit is growing, but not ready for gathering just yet.

☐ **All I seem to produce are dry leaves.**

☐ **I don't have a connection with the vine.**

☐ _____

In biblical imagery, fruit serves two purposes. First, it provides unmistakable proof of identity. Until a tree bears fruit, an untrained eye will have difficulty telling whether it is an apple tree or a pear tree. But if its branches hang heavy with pears, no one can mistake the tree's identity. Second, a full harvest of fruit is an unmistakable sign of health of the tree. Even a novice in horticulture knows that lots of lush, delicious fruit can come only from a strong, vibrant plant.

The interpretation of John 15:6 is a topic of considerable debate among scholars. Some have suggested that the one who "does not abide in Me" is a believer who has failed to be faithful and has lost his or her salvation. But this interpretation contradicts the unmistakable message of Jesus in John 10:27–29 that no one can be saved and then unsaved. Salvation is forever assured by grace through faith in Jesus Christ. Others propose that the one who "does not abide" was never a genuine believer—such as those who reject Jesus entirely or those who merely profess to know Him but don't, like Judas. But the context of Jesus's entire illustration is limited to believers. We know this because John 15:2 speaks of every branch as being "in Me," which presumes a relationship exists, and because 15:3 specifies Jesus's audience as those who are "already clean."

Perhaps an Old Testament passage that Jesus and His disciples knew so well will further illumine our understanding of this verse.

Read Ezekiel 15:1–5. What two kinds of wood does Ezekiel compare?

_____

_____

_____

A tree can be chopped down and the wood used for other purposes. What can a vine be used for once it has been cut away?

_____

_____

_____

Imagine you were stranded in a desert and needed to build a campfire. What kinds of things would you choose to keep the flame going? You would very likely choose things that were the most expendable, the least valuable. You would be foolish to feed your clothing or your map to the flames! Something is usually taken away and burned only when it is good for nothing else. Perhaps Jesus's comment in John 15:6 means simply, *Vinedressers toss disconnected branches aside because dead, dried up branches are good for nothing.* Bible scholar Warren Wiersbe wrote:

> It is unwise to build a theological doctrine on a parable or allegory. Jesus was teaching one main truth—the fruitful life of the believer—and we must not press the details too much. Just as an unfruitful branch is useless, so an unfruitful believer is useless; and both must be dealt with. It is a tragic thing for a once-fruitful believer to backslide and lose his privilege of fellowship and service.[4]

THE HARVEST

Fortunately, branches that maintain their vital link to the vine can enjoy a much brighter future.

Read John 15:7–10.

What does the Lord promise in 15:7?
    Ask _____,
    and _____.

Upon what two conditions does this promise depend?
If you _____,
and _____.

What do you think it means to have Christ's Word abiding in us?

_____

_____

What did Jesus say will glorify God the Father (15:8)?

_____

_____

Jesus said, "Abide in My love" (15:9). How does a believer do that?

_____

STARTING YOUR JOURNEY

When a believer abides in Christ, he or she begins to bear the fruit of a Christ-like character, and the result is a transformed mind (Romans 12:1) that is in harmony with the mind of the Father. The one who abides in Christ can genuinely claim to have "the mind of Christ" (1 Corinthians 2:16). His values become our values. His priorities replace our own. We willingly trade our desires for His. So when we exist in this intimate union, we see at least four other results.

First, *prayers are answered.* This is not to suggest that God will give us just anything we want—health and wealth for us, pain and misery for people we don't like—but we can expect positive answers to prayers offered "in His name" and according to His will. In other words, as we pray for the kinds of things that Jesus would pray for, we can expect results.

Second, *God is glorified.* As we model the character of Jesus, obeying His commands in the same way He obeyed those of the Father, the triune God receives glory. He delights to see us reflecting His character.

Third, *love is stimulated.* As we abide in Christ, the character qualities that honor the Lord begin to emerge, like grapes naturally growing from a healthy, vine-connected branch. Because God is love (1 John 4:8), others will notice this divine quality in our demeanors.

Fourth, *joy will overflow.* Joy doesn't refer to superficial happiness or fleeting cheerfulness. Joy is a deeply felt contentment that transcends difficult circumstances and derives maximum enjoyment from every good experience. As the saying goes, "Joy is the flag that flies over the castle of our hearts, announcing that the King is in residence."[5]

"Abiding in Christ" is admittedly an abstract concept that defies description. Any attempt to explain or illustrate it will be incomplete, inadequate, and potentially misunderstood. Nevertheless, the believer is not only invited, but commanded to remain in an obedient relationship with Christ. As we do that, we will find the comfort, peace, and fulfillment we long for. And we will bear fruit of eternal significance.

Part 3

The Substitute

(Passion)

Lesson 11

The Gathering Storm

SELECTED SCRIPTURES

THE HEART OF THE MATTER

While Jesus was indeed gentle and kind, He also took a bold stand against sin. In fact, when confronting evil dressed in the garb of religion, His formidable anger took many by surprise. He sharply rebuked the religious leaders in Israel for turning their privileged status into an opportunity to gain wealth and power. And from the example of Jesus, we learn how to stand up for the truth, even as we lose popularity and suffer persecution for doing what is right.

DISCOVERING THE WAY

Very often, people portray Jesus as the meek and mild teacher who taught His followers to love others as themselves, to avoid retaliation by turning the other cheek, to pursue peace, and to avoid judging others. While Jesus did indeed possess these qualities and teach these values, the picture is incomplete. The following passages reveal that Jesus was more than the pale, languid figure often portrayed in art, on television, and in movies.

Read Matthew 15:1–14.

What complaint did the religious authorities have against Jesus and His disciples?

_____

_____

What authority did they say Jesus and His disciples had defied?

_____

_____

What authority did Jesus say the Pharisees and scribes had defied?

_____

_____

DOORWAY TO HISTORY
The Roots of Ritual

Many centuries before the earthly ministry of Jesus, the Jewish people were conquered by the Babylonians and carried off to Babylon as slaves. With their temple destroyed and their homeland colonized by other cultures, the Jews looked to the Law of Moses to sustain their national identity and to maintain their distinctiveness as God's chosen people.

In order to help them apply the Law to everyday life in their new and unfamiliar home, teachers of the Jewish Scriptures wrote very careful, specific instructions for the people to follow.

However, what began as a practical aid for contentious Jews became a sacred tradition that took on a life of its own. For instance, ceremonial washing of the hands became an end in itself. Stone water jars were kept ready for use before every meal. A special glass measure was used to draw a small amount from the jars, just enough to fill about one and a half egg-shells. The water was first poured on both hands, the fingers pointing upward, as it flowed over the wrists. If the water stopped short of the wrists, the hands remained unclean. And if it ran down the fingers again, the hands became unclean again, for the water was now itself unclean. Next, each hand was cleansed by being rubbed with the fist of the other.[1] A very devout Jew would undertake this process not only before a meal, but also between each of the courses of the meal.

The body of sacred traditions developed by "the elders" eventually supplanted the very Law it was intended to uphold. And by the time of Jesus, failure to observe tradition was regarded as disobedience to the Law of God. Furthermore, this manmade religiosity became the means by which many Pharisees maintained the illusion of moral superiority over others. Ironically, their religious zeal put them at odds with God. Not only were they motivated by a lust for power, their traditions very often violated the very Law they supposedly cherished.

God is not impressed by religious fervor or hollow adherence to rules. He wants people to do what is right because they are motivated by love for Him.

Jesus applied the words of the prophet Isaiah when speaking to the religious leaders in Matthew 15:7–9. What was his opinion of their religious practices?

Why do you think the disciples were afraid after the encounter? Describe Jesus's attitude.

Later in His ministry, Jesus publicly condemned the religious system in Jerusalem and exposed the moral bankruptcy of the men who ran it.

Read Matthew 23:1–12.

Reading between the lines, what motivated the religious leaders to behave as they did?

_____

_____

Was Jesus guilty of inciting the people to revolution? Why, or why not? What did He tell them to do?

_____

_____

_____

Read Matthew 23:13–33.
In the original language, _woe_ is an interjection that expresses the outrage or the sorrow of the speaker upon seeing the suffering of another.[2] Jesus punctuated each count of His indictment with a "woe," and then He addressed the scribes and Pharisees directly.

How many "woes" did Jesus utter? _____

How many times did He call the scribes and Pharisees "hypocrites"?
_____

How many times did He call them "blind"? _____

To what disparaging images did Jesus liken the hypocritical religious leaders?

_____

_____

_____

During the time of Jesus's earthly ministry, worship in the Jerusalem temple had become big business for religious leaders. The chief priests refused to accept any currency except shekels minted in Israel. Money changers within the temple precincts gladly exchanged any currency for Jewish shekels at an inflated rate and then pocketed the difference. Furthermore, the Law of Moses stated that any animal offered to God had to be flawless; only the best would do. So the men running the temple would inspect the animals brought for sacrifice, ostensibly to verify that the offerings were worthy. However, this was nothing more than a ruse. They arbitrarily rejected animals so that they could offer a suitable replacement in exchange for a fee. Ironically, the "suitable" animal offered for exchange had, only moments before, been the unsuitable sacrifice of another worshipper!

Considering the abuses and outright crimes the religious leaders committed, do you think Jesus's response was appropriate? Why, or why not?

Read Luke 19:45–48 and 21:37–22:2.

How did Jesus address the abuse taking place in the temple?

What was the response of the religious leaders? What prevented them from acting on their hatred?

Did Jesus know His actions would provoke the leaders to such extremes as conspiring to murder Him (see John 6:64)? Why do you think He continued to act so forcefully?

_____

_____

_____

_____

If you were in Jesus's situation, what reasons might you give for not outing the moneychangers completely or for not sticking around to teach in the temple afterwards (Luke 19:47)?

_____

_____

_____

While Jesus had a soft spot in His heart for people who had been trampled by the world's system, He had little patience for those in religious leadership who neglected or abused others. They had direct access to the truth of God, yet they used their privileged position to hoard wealth and power. Make no mistake, they knew what they were doing. And when Jesus boldly exposed their rebellion, it put Him on a collision course with evil.

 STARTING YOUR JOURNEY

Obviously, not every encounter with wrongdoing should be met with such outrage and passion. Jesus encountered evil in many different forms, and He often responded with compassion for the sinner. Nevertheless, even when Jesus took a more gentle approach, He was always fearless and direct.

Not every encounter with wrongdoing should be confronted. However, sometimes it is unavoidable. Describe a situation in which you feel you should take a stand against something you know to be wrong.

What is the morally correct choice?

What opposition or consequences will you face if you stand up for what is right?

Is taking a stand worth it? Why, or why not?

As we determine to take our own stand against evil, four principles emerge from the example of Jesus.

First, *remembering your mission helps you navigate through any storm. Stay focused.* It's not enough to know what's wrong with a situation; we must also define what is right. Once we have determined the correct course of action, we must then keep our eyes focused on following it, even if others discourage or persecute us.

Other than Jesus, name someone who championed right in the face of wrong, despite great personal suffering or sacrifice. For what or whom did he or she fight, and what was the result?

_____

_____

Next, *encountering evil requires sword-like confrontation, not peace-keeping compromise. Stay alert.* One early Christian writer likened God's Word to a two-edged sword, "able to judge the thoughts and intentions of the heart" (Hebrews 4:12). In other words, God's truth has a way of cutting to the heart of a matter. When a clear moral issue is at stake, people-pleasing compromise will tempt us to lay aside the sword of truth. However, we must remember to keep our sword pointed at the issue.

In the specific situation you listed earlier, what do you think would happen if you compromised your moral stand to gain the approval of others?

_____

_____

_____

_____

Third, *being bold when there's a principle worth fighting for is worth the risk, even if it offends and results in misunderstanding. Stay strong.* Misunderstanding is the occupational hazard of leadership. Others will certainly misunderstand or even deliberately misconstrue your intentions, cutting to the heart of your (and every person's) basic desire to be liked. Nevertheless, the moral stand you take will be ultimately worth the sacrifice.

Other than Jesus, name a historical figure who weathered the storm of criticism for the sake of his or her moral stand. How has history judged him or her as a result?

Finally, *speaking up for what is right is no guarantee you'll win or gain respect. Stay realistic.* Jesus took a strong stand against the outrageous evil of the religious leaders in Jerusalem and a storm quickly gathered around Him. He understood the risk. In fact, He knew it would lead to His death. He said to the disciples on the eve of His arrest,

> "If I hadn't come and told [the religious leaders] all this in plain language, it wouldn't be so bad. As it is, they have no excuse. Hate me, hate my Father—it's all the same. If I hadn't done what I have done among them, works no one has ever done, they wouldn't be to blame. But they saw the God-signs and hated anyway, both me and my Father. Interesting—they have verified the truth of their own Scriptures where it is written, 'They hated me for no good reason.'" (John 15:22–25 MSG)

Sometimes the evil we face is so firmly entrenched that we will not see its defeat in our lifetime. In fact, the fight may even require us to sacrifice everything, including our lives. But the Lord does not call us to be successful. He calls us to be faithful. Success or failure is ultimately His responsibility. Ours is to be sure we stand on the correct side of the issue.

When faced with taking a stand for what is right, our greatest temptation is to remain neutral, to forfeit moral leadership for sake of popularity. Certainly, we should choose our battles wisely and be sure of our motives before we take a stand. But we cannot allow the approval of others to outweigh faithfulness to God and the truth He loves so much. Like Jesus, we must stand up for the truth, even if we lose popularity and suffer persecution for doing what is right.

Lesson 12

Betrayed and Arrested

SELECTED SCRIPTURES

THE HEART OF THE MATTER

Perhaps no name in history is more synonymous with *traitor* than Judas. He enjoyed the spiritual, mental, and emotional benefits of a close association with the Lord as one of His twelve select men. He was mentored, empowered, and groomed for leadership. He saw Jesus's miracles and heard His teaching. He was even entrusted with the management of the group's money. Nevertheless, unresolved, secret sin turned the inner Judas into a very different man than the one his friends knew. But Jesus was not fooled. The story of Judas teaches us that no one is immune to the insidious, corrosive power of secret sin.

DISCOVERING THE WAY

As Jesus carried out His ministry of teaching and healing, He attracted a large number of followers. From them, He selected an inner circle of twelve men to groom for leadership (Matthew 10:1–10). One of the twelve was a young man named Judas Iscariot. Some scholars see in Judas's surname a possible clue to his past. *Iscariot* sounds like it could be connected with the Greek term *sikarios,* or "dagger-bearer." In Acts 21:38, the term refers to the followers of an Egyptian revolutionary. William Barclay's work *The Master's Men* gives additional insight.

The *sicarii* were wild and fanatical nationalists, pledged not only to war against the Romans, but to murder and assassination at every opportunity. If this is so, and it is by no means impossible, Judas was a violent Jewish nationalist, who had attached himself to Jesus in the hope that through Jesus his nationalist dreams might be realized.[1]

Many of Jesus's followers outside the twelve had similar designs. They hoped He would be the king who would free them from the tyranny of Rome (John 6:15). But Jesus made it very clear that His mission did not include raising an army to win independence for Israel. Rather, He had come to give them (and us) spiritual victory over sin.

 Read John 6:14–15, 66–71.

How did many of Jesus's followers respond to His refusal to become their military leader?

_____

_____

Peter presumed to speak for those who remained. What reason did he give for continuing to follow Jesus?

_____

_____

Why do you think the writer, John, foreshadowed Judas's betrayal at this point in the story?

_____

_____

After this incident, the twelve disciples continued to travel with Jesus, hearing Him teach and watching Him exercise power over sickness, demons, the weather, and even death. All the while, Jesus groomed His hand-selected team of twelve for ministry. During this time, perhaps the seeds of disappointment sown earlier in Judas's spirit had begun to germinate. It seems clear that one particular situation brought his discontent to full flower.

 Read Mark 14:1–11 (see also Matthew 26:14–16 and John 12:1–8).

As Jesus and the disciples prepared to celebrate Passover, what did His enemies do?

_____

_____

What prevented them from carrying out their plan? (Mark 14:2; see also John 12:9–15)

_____

_____

What occurred in the meantime that caused Judas Iscariot to be embarrassed in public?

_____

_____

 Read Matthew 26:14–16.

What did Judas do immediately after this event?

_____

_____

How much money did Judas receive to betray his Master?

_____

What does this suggest was going on within Judas during his association with Jesus? (See also John 12:6.)

_____

_____

Read Luke 22:1–6 and John 12:1–8.

What additional detail does Luke's account provide concerning Judas's state of mind? (Luke 22:3)

_____

_____

How do you think Judas's growing resentment and the involvement of Satan were related?

_____

_____

Following the incident in which Judas was publicly rebuked and after he had met with the religious leaders, the twelve disciples gathered to enjoy the Passover meal with Jesus. During the meal, Jesus announced that one of the men in the room would soon betray Him. When one of the disciples asked who would do something so unthinkable, Jesus privately indicated that it would be Judas. John's account reveals that Satan was again involved in Judas's actions (John 13:21–30). The disciple quietly slipped out of the room to carry out his heinous plan.

Jesus knew it would be His last evening with the remaining eleven men, so He took great care to teach them and prepare them for the awful ordeal that would soon begin. He suggested the group spend the rest of the evening at a familiar retreat, a garden called Gethsemane on the Mount of Olives, just east of Jerusalem.

After a long, agonizing night spent in prayer, Jesus announced to the remaining eleven disciples that the ordeal He had predicted many times was about to begin.

 Read Matthew 26:47–50.

Jesus: The Greatest Life of All

Whom did Judas lead to the garden?

What prearranged signal did he use to identify Jesus for the mob?

The word translated as "kissed" in Matthew 26:49 means "to kiss fervently."[2] "The compound verb has the force of an *emphatic, ostentatious* salute."[3] We might paraphrase the sentence to read, "And he fell on Him with kisses." It's the same word used in Luke 15:20 to describe the greeting the Prodigal Son received from his father upon returning home.

Why do you think Judas chose to make such a display instead of simply saying, "This is the man"?

When Jesus responded, what did He call Judas? Why do you think Jesus did this?

As soon as Jesus was identified for the mob, He was seized without a struggle and delivered to temple authorities. Judas's betrayal was the catalyst for the trials and execution of Jesus, which will be the subject of the next three lessons. But for Judas, this marked the beginning of his own demise.

Read Matthew 27:3–10.

114

How did Judas feel about his actions once Jesus had been condemned to death?

_____

_____

Obviously, Judas considered thirty pieces of silver (about one month's wages for a skilled laborer) to be a fair sum before the betrayal. What was his opinion of the money afterward?

_____

_____

What words or actions in this passage suggest that Judas's opinion of Jesus had changed?

_____

_____

What words or actions in this passage suggest that Judas's feelings and words were genuinely remorseful?

_____

_____

In death, Judas failed to make the necessary connection between remorse and repentance, just as he had in life. The years he spent with Jesus had taught him nothing. His tragic choice to end his life rather than to ask for forgiveness merely consummated the hypocritical double life he had cultivated from the beginning. In the end, Judas died as he had lived. He loved his sin.

STARTING YOUR JOURNEY

The Bible never tells a story merely for the sake of entertainment. Even the wretched double life of Judas has much to teach us. His negative example illustrates four key principles we would do well to keep in mind as we contemplate our own spiritual lives.

First, *association with godliness is no guarantee that we will become godly.* Joining a healthy church and cultivating relationships with spiritually mature people should be a priority. We need healthy influences. However, associating with mature believers will not nourish the soul any more than merely sitting in a restaurant will nourish the body. To grow wise and to develop spiritually, we must personally take in what Jesus offers. We each must study His Word and submit to its truth.

Second, *moral corruption in secret is more deadly than visible moral corruption.* No cancer is more deadly than the one that goes undetected. The same is true of sin. Keeping our sinful nature carefully concealed keeps us from applying the remedy of forgiveness Jesus provided through the gift of salvation. One of His disciples later wrote, "If we confess our sins, He is faithful and righteous to forgive us our sins and to cleanse us from all unrighteousness" (1 John 1:9). Failure to confess and receive forgiveness forces us to cope with the deadly effects of sin in ways that are sure to cause more damage later. In the case of Judas, his secret affair with sin consumed and ultimately destroyed him.

Each of us has a dark side we would prefer to keep hidden from others. How do you deal with yours?

How well does this work for you? Which do you feel as time goes by, greater freedom or increased burden?

Take a moment to sit quietly and ask God to show you whether you are harboring secret sin. Are you? How is it affecting your life?

According to 1 John 1:9, how does one go about bringing secret sin into the light?

_____

_____

Next, *Satan and his demons are looking for any opportunity to work against the Lord.* Several passages of Scripture teach that the person who bears unresolved sin is an ideal vessel by which the devil may attack the people and plans of God (Genesis 4:6–7; Ephesians 4:25–27; 5:15–16; 1 Peter 5:6–8). At first, the person appears to be immune from the consequences of his or her sin, but after Satan has done all the damage he can do, the vessel is consumed by the sin that carried it.

Choose to be a vessel suitable for the good things God wants you to enjoy. If you are carrying unresolved sin, please take time to read "Clearing Away the Clutter of Unresolved Sin" at the back of this book.

Finally, *no sorrow can compare to the remorse of one who discovers too late that he or she has misunderstood Jesus and spurned His love.* Satan's primary tool is deception, which he uses to twist unresolved sin and selfish motivation to serve his purposes. And once he is finished using someone, he cruelly unmasks the truth to reveal the consequences of that person's foolish choices. The flood of shame, humiliation, regret, self-condemnation, and hopelessness can be overwhelming.

Fortunately, Jesus continues to say, "If you continue in My word, then you are truly disciples of Mine; and you will know the truth, and the truth will make you free" (John 8:31–32).

Is there any reason why you feel you cannot trust the Lord enough to submit to His truth and ask for His forgiveness? If so, you are not alone. Many people struggle with this decision. Use the space below to describe the reason for your reluctance.

_____

_____

_____

_____

_____

_____

Now you must take a step of faith. Take what you wrote above and give it to the Lord, trusting Him to resolve it on your behalf. The only way to personally discover the love of God is to put it to the test. To begin to take this important step, personalize the sample prayer below.

> My Heavenly Father,
>
> I confess that I am reluctant to trust You because of (state the reason you described above). I also admit that I have unresolved sin in my life. I humbly ask your forgiveness, and I submit myself to Your sovereign care for instruction and healing. Do whatever You deem necessary to cure me and teach me how to choose better.
> I ask this of you in the name of Your Son, Jesus.
>
> Amen.

Judas will forever be remembered as the most heinous traitor of all time. However, we are foolish to think that his story cannot become ours. Despite all the advantages he enjoyed as a close associate of Jesus, the promising, young disciple became a monster. And if we think we could never become something so despicable, we have failed to hear and heed the warning of Scripture. Secret sin is an indiscriminant killer, and those who think they are immune are often the most vulnerable of all.

Lesson 13

Analysis of a Courtroom Fiasco

SELECTED SCRIPTURES

THE HEART OF THE MATTER

Jesus was the only person to live His entire life without doing anything wrong. Yet, He was arrested, tried, convicted, and condemned to suffer a punishment normally reserved for the Roman Empire's worst criminals. His arrest was a betrayal and His trials a farce, His convictions illegal and His punishment a travesty of justice. Yet through it all, He remained calm, He answered questions honestly, He spoke the truth with dignity, and He calmly resolved to allow the Father to vindicate Him at the proper time. We would do well to imitate Christ in our response to the injustices we experience in our lives.

DISCOVERING THE WAY

After celebrating the Passover meal with His disciples, Jesus suggested they walk to their familiar retreat on the Mount of Olives, a private garden called Gethsemane. Jesus knew that Judas was carrying out his treacherous plan to betray Him to Israel's religious leaders and He also knew that He was beginning a long, torturous ordeal which would lead to an agonizing death on a cross. He spent His last night of freedom praying for courage to quell the overwhelming feeling of dread and for strength to endure the coming trial with dignity. But most of all, Jesus was praying for the Father's sovereign plan to prevail.

Sometime during the night, a cohort of Roman soldiers (typically 600 trained men)[1] and several Jewish officers quietly surrounded the garden. Judas then greeted his Master with a smile and a profusion of kisses, signaling to the assailants hidden in the shadows. While the religious leaders came prepared for a fight, Jesus offered no resistance, even suppressing Peter's impulse to take on the small army with his dagger. A few simple words reveal Jesus's perspective, helping us understand how He could endure the outrageous injustices of the next several hours: "The cup which the Father has given Me, shall I not drink it?" (John 18:11).

The assault at Gethsemane set in motion a series of six trials; three before the Jewish religious authorities and three before the civil authorities of Rome. In this lesson, we will examine the first three trials of Jesus. His appearances before Pilate and Herod Antipas will be the subject of Lesson 14.

First-century Israelites were a law-conscious people and they maintained a strict procedure for hearing civil and criminal cases. A document called the *Mishnah*, compiled around AD 200, records the oral traditions handed down by the Jewish people from one generation to another over several centuries. A portion of this document describes the guidelines that governed the Jewish ruling council, called the Sanhedrin, which was responsible for hearing cases, rendering judgment, and passing sentence on the guilty. This document very likely describes the traditions that governed the Sanhedrin during the time of Jesus.

A chart listing some of the rules in the *Mishah* is provided on the pages that follow. As you study the biblical accounts of the trials of Jesus, use it as a measure to examine and critique the judicial process that tried and convicted Jesus.

Mishnah: Sanhedrin Guidelines for Capital Cases

	Rule	Primary Source	Secondary Source	Actual Practice
#1	No trials were to occur during the night hours (before the morning sacrifice).	Mishnah: Sanhedrin 4:1	Laurna L. Berg, "The Illegalities of Jesus' Religious and Civil Trials," (Bibliotheca Sacra, Vol. 161, No. 643, July - September, 2004), 330 - 342	Jesus was taken to Annas, Caiaphas, and the Sanhedrin at night.
#2	Trials were not to occur on the eve of a Sabbath or during festivals.	Mishnah: Sanhedrin 4:1	Laurna L. Berg, "The Illegalities of Jesus' Religious and Civil Trials," (Bibliotheca Sacra, Vol. 161, No. 643, July - September, 2004), 330 - 342	The trials occurred at night during the Passover celebration.
#3	All trials were to be public; secret trials were forbidden.	Mishnah: Sanhedrin 1:6	Laurna L. Berg, "The Illegalities of Jesus' Religious and Civil Trials," (Bibliotheca Sacra, Vol. 161, No. 643, July - September, 2004), 330 - 342	Jesus was taken before the Sanhedrin at night for questioning and was immediately delared "guilty." Only his official sentencing took place during the day.
#4	All trials were to be held in the Hall of Judgment in the temple area.	Mishnah: Sanhedrin 11:2	Laurna L. Berg, "The Illegalities of Jesus' Religious and Civil Trials," (Bibliotheca Sacra, Vol. 161, No. 643, July - September, 2004), 330 - 342	Jesus was first taken to Annas, then Caiaphas before put before the Sanhedrin.
#5	Capital cases required a minimum of twenty-three judges.	Mishnah: Sanhedrin 4:1	Laurna L. Berg, "The Illegalities of Jesus' Religious and Civil Trials," (Bibliotheca Sacra, Vol. 161, No. 643, July - September, 2004), 330 - 342	We don't know how many judges were present. The trials took place at night during a festival.
#6	An accused person could not testify against himself.	Mishnah: Sanhedrin 3:3-4	Laurna L. Berg, "The Illegalities of Jesus' Religious and Civil Trials," (Bibliotheca Sacra, Vol. 161, No. 643, July - September, 2004), 330 - 342	The Sanhedrin convicted Jesus on His own words and did not see the need for witnesses.
#7	Someone was required to speak on behalf of the accused.		Darrell L. Bock, "Jesus v. Sanhedrin: Why Jesus 'lost' his trial," (Christianity Today, Vol. 42, No. 4, April 6, 1998), 49.	No one spoke for Jesus, and when He objected to the illegality of the proceeding, He was struck in the face.
#8	Conviction required the testimony of two or three witnesses to be in perfect alignment.	Deuteronomy 17:6-7, 19:15-20		The prosecution sought witnesses against Jesus, but their testimony conflicted.
#9	Witnesses for the prosecution were to be examined and cross-examined extensively.	Mishnah: Sanhedrin 4:1		Witnesses were sought against Jesus for the purpose of conviction, not to acquit Him or even find the truth.
#10	Capital cases were to follow a strict order, beginning with arguments by the defense, then arguments for conviction.	Mishnah: Sanhedrin 4:1	Laurna L. Berg, "The Illegalities of Jesus' Religious and Civil Trials," (Bibliotheca Sacra, Vol. 161, No. 643, July - September, 2004), 330 - 342	No one spoke in Jesus's defense, neither before the accusations, nor after.
#11	All Sanhedrin judges could argue for aquittal, but not all could argue for conviction.	Mishnah: Sanhedrin 4:1	Laurna L. Berg, "The Illegalities of Jesus' Religious and Civil Trials," (Bibliotheca Sacra, Vol. 161, No. 643, July - September, 2004), 330 - 342	The chief priests and the council sought witnesses against Jesus.

	Rule	Primary Source	Secondary Source	Actual Practice
#12	The High Priest should not participate in the questioning.		Darrell L. Bock, "Jesus v. Sanhedrin: Why Jesus 'lost' his trial," (Christianity Today, Vol. 42, No. 4, April 6, 1998), 49.	Both Annas and Caiaphas interrogated Jesus directly, asking questions designed to incriminate Him.
#13	Each witness in a capital case was to be examined individually, not in the presence of other witnesses.	Mishnah: Sanhedrin 3:6	Laurna L. Berg, "The Illegalities of Jesus' Religious and Civil Trials," (Bibliotheca Sacra, Vol. 161, No. 643, July - September, 2004), 330 - 342	We don't know how many witnesses were brought to testify at any given time.
#14	The testimony of two witnesses found to be in contradiction rendered both invalid.	Mishnah: Sanhedrin 5:2	Laurna L. Berg, "The Illegalities of Jesus' Religious and Civil Trials," (Bibliotheca Sacra, Vol. 161, No. 643, July - September, 2004), 330 - 342	The testimonies of those who testified against Jesus did not agree.
#15	Voting for conviction and sentencing in a capital case to be conducted individually, beginning with the youngest, so younger members would not be influenced by the voting of the elder members.	Mishnah: Sanhedrin 4:2	Laurna L. Berg, "The Illegalities of Jesus' Religious and Civil Trials," (Bibliotheca Sacra, Vol. 161, No. 643, July - September, 2004), 330 - 342	The members of the Sanhedrin voted simultaneously and nearly rioted.
#16	Verdicts in capital cases were to be handed down only during daylight hours.	Mishnah: Sanhedrin 4:1	Laurna L. Berg, "The Illegalities of Jesus' Religious and Civil Trials," (Bibliotheca Sacra, Vol. 161, No. 643, July - September, 2004), 330 - 342	The Sanhedrin convicted Jesus and condemned Him right away, then reconvened the next day to give the appearance of order.
#17	The members of the Sanhedrin were to meet in pairs all night, discuss the case, and reconvene for the purpose of confirming the final verdict and imposing sentence.	Mishnah: Sanhedrin 4:1		We see only a rush to judgment and no indication that the judges met for any reason, least of all to find Jesus "not guilty."
#18	Sentencing in a capital case was not to occur until the following day.	Mishnah: Sanhedrin 4:1	Laurna L. Berg, "The Illegalities of Jesus' Religious and Civil Trials," (Bibliotheca Sacra, Vol. 161, No. 643, July - September, 2004), 330 - 342	The Sanhedrin convicted Jesus and condemned Him right away, then reconvened the next day to give the appearance of order.

THE FIRST TRIAL

 Read John 18:12–24.

To whom was Jesus first taken, and what was this person's relationship to the high priest of Israel?

Skim John 18:1–11. At what time of day does it appear that this hearing took place?

_____

_____

According to the chart, which of the Sanhedrin's own rules did Annas break in 18:19?

_____

_____

In His response to Annas, Jesus encouraged him to follow certain rules of jurisprudence (18:20–21). Which specific rules do you think He had in mind?

_____

_____

_____

_____

How would you describe Jesus's attitude and demeanor toward Annas and the others during this hearing?

_____

_____

DOORWAY TO HISTORY

The Annas Crime Family

During the first century, the high priest in Israel held essentially the same type of authority as a king; however, his appointment had to be approved by Rome and he governed under the authority of the Roman procurator. Though Caiaphas officially held the office, many recognized his father-in-law, Annas, as the true power behind the office.

Annas was originally appointed high priest in AD 6 by Quirinius, the governor of Syria, but he was later deposed by Valerius Gratus in AD 15. Nevertheless, he remained the head of a vast empire of organized corruption in Jerusalem; "He and his family were proverbial for their rapacity and greed."[2] After his removal from office, he wielded power through his son, Eleazar, and then through his son-in-law, Caiaphas. In fact, his family held a virtually unbroken line of succession through four more sons after Caiaphas and then a grandson.

In addition to enjoying the benefits of Sadducean aristocracy, Annas held a monopoly on animals deemed acceptable for sacrifice in the temple. If a worshiper's animal was found to be insufficient, a new, suitable one had to be purchased. These Annas sold "in the four famous 'booths of the sons of Annas' on the Mt. of Olives, with a branch within the precincts of the temple itself."[3] According to the Law of Moses, the priests were to determine which animals were of sufficient quality for sacrifice. And, of course, Annas controlled the priests.

Soon after Jesus cleansed the temple of what He called "a robbers' den," several religious authorities demanded to know, "By what authority are You doing these things, and who gave You this authority?" (Matthew 21:23). Understandably, they could not imagine one man challenging the Annas crime family without the backing of someone immensely powerful.

A casual observer might have been impressed by the religious zeal of Caiaphas, who "tore his robes and said, 'He has blasphemed!'" (Matthew 26:65) when Jesus claimed to be the Messiah. In reality Caiaphas and Annas wanted Jesus dead for two other reasons. First, Jesus dared to defy the high priest's sovereign control over the temple. Second—and more importantly—Jesus was bad for business.

THE SECOND TRIAL

 Read Mark 14:53–65.

To whom was Jesus taken next? What office did this individual hold? (See also John 18:24.)

_____

_____

"Trying to obtain testimony against Jesus to put Him to death" (Mark 14:55) was a violation of which parts of the *Mishnah*, specifically? (see chart on pages 114–115, if necessary.)

_____

_____

How did the false testimony (14:56–57) differ from the truth?

_____

_____

According to the *Mishnah*, how should the Sanhedrin have responded to the false testimony?

_____

_____

When Caiaphas questioned Jesus, which rules did he violate? And which rules did the Sanhedrin violate in their rush to judgment?

_____

_____

The trial described in Mark 14:53–65 (see also Matthew 26:57–68 and John 18:24) took place immediately after Jesus's hearing before Annas, so it stands to reason that it took place at night. As the second trial concluded, the members of the Sanhedrin and others in attendance vented their anger on Jesus before retiring for the night.

THE THIRD TRIAL

 Read Mark 15:1 and Luke 22:66–71.

Review the Sanhedrin's rules on the chart on pages 114–115. Why do you think the religious authorities assembled the next day?

_____

_____

Do you think their actions reflected a genuine desire to carry out justice? Why, or why not?

_____

_____

How did Jesus behave when He was read the verdict? Was He respectful? Did He avoid speaking the truth?

_____

_____

How difficult do you think it was for Him to respond this way after the injustice, humiliation, and abuse He had suffered the night before?

_____

_____

For a detailed study of Jesus's trials, read each of the primary passages describing the trials of Jesus (Matthew 26:57–68; Mark 14:53–15:1; Luke 22:66–71; John 18:12–24) and complete the chart titled "Sanhedrin Trial Scorecard" at the end of this lesson.

Ultimately, Jesus was found guilty of calling Himself "the Christ" (Matthew 26:63), the long-awaited Jewish Messiah. Was He innocent of this charge?

_____

_____

Why did the council of elders consider this to be a threat? (See John 11:47–53.)

_____

_____

The religious authorities had some problems to solve if they were to rid themselves of Jesus. They were "not permitted to put anyone to death" (John 18:31); Rome reserved capital punishment for its own use. The Empire had two prevailing interests in any given region: peaceful submission to Roman authority and the steady flow of taxes into Rome. It generally avoided involvement in local squabbles unless something threatened these two primary concerns. So, the religious authorities needed to convince Roman officials that executing Jesus would serve the interests of the government. And perhaps more important, Jesus was an immensely popular teacher. Due to thier fear of the people's response, the religious authorities had to discredit Him in order to avoid widespread dissent when Rome executed Jesus.

By the end of the third trial, the religious leaders had what they felt they needed. Jesus claimed to be the Christ, the one whom Jews widely regarded as their hope of expelling their Roman oppressors. Certainly, the Empire would want to rid itself of a potential revolutionary, and if Jesus *were* executed by the Romans, the people would reject Him as just another false messiah. It was an ideal solution that brought together an unlikely alliance of Pharisees (scribes and lay teachers), Sadducees (priests), and Zealots (underground revolutionaries). These enemies found common ground to destroy a common enemy: God's Son.

STARTING YOUR JOURNEY

The rules of the Sanhedrin had, for generations, safeguarded the innocent from false accusations. To that end, the Sanhedrin acted not only as judge and jury, but also as counsel for the defense. But in the case of *The Sanhedrin v. Jesus*, something went terribly wrong and the trials became a courtroom fiasco.

But Jesus's trials were the machinations of corrupt men jealously guarding their power. And to make matters worse, they draped their outrageous behavior in the august robes of religious purity.

The religious authorities successfully cast Jesus in the role of villain and accepted the applause and even the admiration of an unwary public. They successfully covered their tracks so that no one could see their impropriety, their lust for power, and their shameful conspiracy to destroy an innocent. Nor did the Jewish people comprehend the astounding blessings they were forfeiting by killing their Messiah.

Describe a time when you suffered an injustice.

_____

_____

How did it affect your reputation? Your relationships with others?

_____

_____

How did it feel to consider that the person or people responsible for the injustice could escape the consequences of wrongdoing?

_____

_____

How did you respond to the situation?

_____

_____

Very few situations in life are more frustrating than suffering injustice alone and unnoticed. Outrage demands justice, bitterness demands revenge, hopelessness begs heaven for relief, and loneliness cries out to be heard as a watching world stands aloof. During those dark, painful, lonely times, the silence from heaven can be deafening.

If this is presently your experience, rest assured, you are not alone. The Lord does see your suffering, and He will not allow it to go unanswered. He will see that justice is done, though probably not at the time or in the manner you would like. Nevertheless, the agony you suffer will not go to waste. If you go through it, this experience can be the means by which God brings you His greatest blessings.

Stop trying to be heard and stop striving for vindication. Speak the truth—in love and without apology—to the appropriate parties. And submit yourself to the sovereign will of God, understanding that He may also be using the situation to give you a needed dose of humility.

Jesus accepted that He would not receive justice from men. He knew that the world was dominated by sin and governed by corrupt people. He did not look to the courts for justice or to the people for approval and affirmation. Instead He submitted Himself to the will of the Father. He spoke the truth and refused to allow anger or bitterness to distract anyone from seeing it. He entrusted Himself to the One who will ultimately and inevitably judge every soul righteously.

Sanhedrin Trial Scorecard

Review the primary passages that describe the trials of Jesus and indicate which rules were violated by placing a check in the appropriate box.

Rule		Trial #1: Annas (John 18:12–23)	Trial #2: Caiaphas & Sanhedrin (Matthew 26:57–68; Mark 14:53–65; John 18:24)	Trial #3: Sanhedrin (Mark 15:1; Luke 22:66–71)
#1	No trials were to occur during the night hours (before the morning sacrifice).			
#2	Trials were not to occur on the eve of a Sabbath or during festivals.			
#3	All trials were to be public; secret trials were forbidden.			
#4	All trials were to be held in the Hall of Judgment in the temple area.			
#5	Capital cases required a minimum of twenty-three judges.			
#6	An accused person could not testify against himself.			
#7	Someone was required to speak on behalf of the accused.			
#8	Conviction required the testimony of two or three witnesses to be in perfect alignment.			
#9	Witnesses for the prosecution were to be examined and cross-examined extensively.			
#10	Capital cases were to follow a strict order, beginning with arguments by the defense, then arguments for conviction.			

Sanhedrin Trial Scorecard (Cont.)

Review the primary passages that describe the trials of Jesus and indicate which rules were violated by placing a check in the appropriate box.	Trial #1: Annas (John 18:12–23)	Trial #2: Caiaphas & Sanhedrin (Matthew 26:57–68; Mark 14:53–65; John 18:24)	Trial #3: Sanhedrin (Mark 15:1; Luke 22:66–71)
Rule			
#11 All Sanhedrin judges could argue for aquittal, but not all could argue for conviction.			
#12 The High Priest could not participate in the questioning.			
#13 Each witness in a capital case was to be examined individually, not in the presence of other witnesses.			
#14 The testimony of two witnesses found to be in contradiction rendered both invalid.			
#15 Voting for conviction and sentencing in a capital case was to be conducted individually, beginning with the youngest, so younger members would not be influenced by the voting of the elder members.			
#16 Verdicts in capital cases were to be handed down only during daylight hours.			
#17 The members of the Sanhedrin were to meet in pairs all night, discuss the case, and reconvene for the purpose of confirming the final verdict and imposing sentence.			
#18 Sentencing in a capital case was not to occur until the following day.			

Lesson 14

The Last Trials and Torture of Jesus

THE HEART OF THE MATTER

The Apostle's Creed states that Jesus "suffered under Pontius Pilate,"[1] which is certainly true; however, many people had a hand in the unjust conviction of Jesus. Pilate washed his hands of the truth. Herod treated Jesus like an idle curiosity. Pilate's wife regarded Jesus with fear and superstition. And the angry mob rejected Jesus because He was not the Messiah-King they wanted.

While the trials of Jesus adjourned more than two millennia ago, each of us must render a verdict in our own hearts. Only now, it is not His fate we decide. It is our own.

DISCOVERING THE WAY

After three religious trials, the Sanhedrin found a charge to pin on Jesus, a charge that they were counting on to shift popular opinion away from His supporters and clear the way to have Jesus put to death. Now the Sanhedrin needed to convince their Roman overseer that executing Jesus would be good for Caesar and the Roman Empire. Delivering Jesus to Pontius Pilate began a series of three trials before the civil authorities of Rome. The following chart provides an overview of all of the trials Jesus faced.

The Trials of Jesus

Trial	Officiating Authority	Scripture	Accusations	Legality	Type	Result
1	Annas, former High Priest from AD 6–15	John 18:12–23	No specific charges were brought.	Illegal: No jurisdiction Held at night No charges No witnesses Abused during trial	Jewish and Religious	Jesus was found "guilty" of irreverence and sent to Caiaphas.
2	Caiaphas, High Priest from AD 18–36, and the Sanhedrin	Matthew 26:57–68 Mark 14:53–65 John 18:24	Jesus claimed to be the Messiah, the Son of God, which they deemed blasphemy.	Illegal: Held at night False witnesses No formal charge Abused during trial	Jewish and Religious	Jesus was declared "guilty" of blasphemy and held for sentencing until morning.
3	The Sanhedrin	Mark 15:1 Luke 22:66–71	As a continuation of the earlier trial before the Sanhedrin, the charges remained the same.	Illegal: Accusation changed No witnesses Improper vote	Jewish and Religious	Jesus was sentenced to be turned over to Romans for execution.
4	Pontius Pilate, Governor of Judea from AD 26–36	Matthew 27:11–14 Mark 15:2–5 Luke 23:1–7 John 18:28–38	Jesus was charged with treason and sedition against Rome.	Illegal: Found "not guilty," yet kept in custody No defense representation Abused during trial	Roman and Civil	Jesus was declared "not guilty" and pawned off on Herod Antipas to find a loophole.
5	Herod Antipas, Governor of Galilee from 4 BC–AD 39	Luke 23:8–12	No specific charges were brought. Jesus was questioned at length by Herod.	Illegal: No jurisdiction No specific charges Abused during trial	Roman and Civil	Jesus was mistreated, mocked, falsely accused, and returned to Pilate without a decision made.
6	Pontius Pilate	Matthew 27:15–26 Mark 15:6–15 Luke 23:13–25 John 18:39–19:16	As a continuation of the earlier trial before Pilate, the charges remained the same.	Illegal: Declared "not guilty," yet condemned	Roman and Civil	Jesus was declared "not guilty" but sentenced to be crucified to mollify the angry mob. Simultaneously, a man guilty of murder, treason, and sedition was released.

As the procurator appointed by Rome to govern the region of Judea, Pontius Pilate was required to hear and render a verdict on all capital cases. Local authorities were not permitted to execute prisoners.

THE FOURTH TRIAL

 Read John 18:28–38 and Luke 23:1–5.

What specific accusations did the religious leaders bring against Jesus?

_____

_____

_____

_____

Were these accusations true or false? (See Luke 20:25–26; 22:67–71.)

_____

_____

Why would the Romans consider the charge, "saying that He Himself is Christ, a King" (Luke 23:2), worthy of execution?

_____

_____

How was the accusation in Luke 23:2 a half-truth? (See Luke 20:22–26.) It was true because:

_____

_____

It was false because:

_____

_____

What was Pilate's initial verdict?

In his account, Luke noted that the religious leaders would not accept Pilate's initial verdict and that the agitation of the crowd put him in a difficult position. The evidence did not support the Jews' claim that Jesus was an insurrectionist, yet Pilate's refusal to execute Him would likely instigate riots. Pilate's primary responsibility was to maintain stability in the region, so imagine the embarrassment he would face in Rome if the people rioted because he protected an accused revolutionary!

As the religious leaders pressed their case against Jesus, they mentioned that His influence extended to Galilee, where He was from. Upon hearing this, Pilate thought he had found an opportunity to toss the political timebomb into someone else's lap. Herod Antipas, the ruler over Galilee, happened to be in Jerusalem for Passover. So Pilate sent Jesus to him.

Herod Antipas was a caricature of Roman dissipation. As the rich son of Herod the Great, he inherited the title of "tetrarch" over Galilee and Peraea, but his rule consisted mostly of self-indulgence and frivolous parties. For example, he consummated an affair with his brother's wife, Herodias, by driving his current wife away and marrying his mistress. His actions not only violated a marriage treaty but flouted Jewish law, drawing criticism from John the Baptist. At one of Herod's parties, the "the daughter of Herodias danced before them and pleased Herod, so much that he promised with an oath to give her whatever she asked" (Matthew 14:6–7). She asked for John's head on a platter, which Herod promptly delivered. This was the sort of man who presided over the next trial of Jesus.

THE FIFTH TRIAL

Read Luke 23:8–12.

Why was Herod Antipas so pleased to have Jesus appear before him?

Herod "questioned Him at some length." Why do you think Jesus remained silent?

What did Herod do instead of hearing arguments and rendering a verdict?

Of what significance was the "gorgeous robe" Herod put on Jesus before returning Him to Pilate?

Herod Antipas had become famous for his rash, politically foolish decisions. Perhaps Pilate thought another would solve his dilemma. After all, Herod had ordered the beheading of John the Baptist at a time when most everyone accepted him as a genuine prophet. But Herod didn't take the bait, and Pilate's dilemma returned to him.

THE SIXTH TRIAL

 Read Luke 23:13–25 and John 18:38–19:15.

What was Pilate's final verdict in the case of *The Sanhedrin v. Jesus?*

Pilate had Jesus scourged. "[Such] punishment was horrible, the victim being bound to a low pillar or stake, and beaten, either with rods, or, in the case of slaves and provincials, with scourges, called *scorpions*, leather thongs tipped with leaden balls or sharp spikes."[2] This punishment very often proved fatal to the victim.

Given the final verdict, why do you think Pilate had Jesus scourged?

_____

_____

In Luke's account how many times does Pilate declare Jesus to be innocent of all charges? How many times in John's?

_____

_____

Pilate grew "even more afraid" (John 18:8) when he discovered that Jesus claimed to be the Son of God. And his conversation with Jesus, recorded in John 18:9–11, only heightened his fear. Matthew's account records another factor that certainly added to Pilate's growing anxiety: "While he was sitting on the judgment seat, his wife sent him a message, saying, 'Have nothing to do with that righteous Man; for last night I suffered greatly in a dream because of Him'" (Matthew 27:19).

Roman religion allowed for a multitude of gods, all of whom needed to be appeased. Consequently, people of that culture were notoriously superstitious, believing almost everything in life to be influenced by good or evil spirits and the supernatural intervention of deities. So, the concern of Pilate's wife about her dream is not surprising. She did not believe in Jesus as the Son of the one-and-only God, but perhaps merely as the physical offspring of a god or someone who was highly favored by a god.

Pilate tried to release Jesus using a certain tradition as a loophole. What was the tradition?

_____

When his tactic backfired, whom was he forced to release instead? What, ironically, was his crime, according to Luke 23:19?

_____

_____

Why did Pilate finally relent and send Jesus to the executioners?

_____

_____

Matthew's account tells us that Pilate "took water and washed his hands in front of the crowd, saying, 'I am innocent of this Man's blood'" (Matthew 27:24). And with that, Jesus was prepared for crucifixion, while another man—one truly guilty of insurrection—went free.

STARTING YOUR JOURNEY
The trials of Jesus feature a cast of four main characters, each of which illustrates a common response to the Son of God—responses we still see today.

Pilate—He was completely convinced by the truth, yet terrified to admit it or act upon it for fear of losing favor with people.

Herod—He was so distracted by superficial pursuits that truth had no appeal.

Pilate's wife—She was so easily persuaded and carelessly undiscerning that truth and fiction commingled with ease.

The religious leaders—They were willfully unconcerned with truth because it frustrated their personal agenda.

Which of these perspectives do you see most often among the people you encounter?

_____

_____

How does it affect their spiritual lives?

_____

_____

_____

How does it affect their manner of living in areas such as making wise choices, being dependable, caring for others?

_____

_____

What is your verdict? Was Jesus who He said He was? How have you responded to Him?

_____

_____

_____

Each of these responses to truth profoundly affects how a person lives and relates to others. They can also prevent someone from seeing the truth about Jesus, accepting the truth about Jesus, or applying the truth about Jesus. Regardless of their response, the eternal consequences are the same. The apostle Paul wrote to a group of Christians living in Ephesus, "By grace you have been saved *through faith*" (Ephesians 2:8, emphasis added).

Faith is essentially the act of placing one's trust in a certain truth and then relying upon that belief. For instance, an airline claims that a particular aircraft is safe for travel. When a traveler boards the plane, he or she hears the statement, accepts the statement as truth, and then acts upon the truth by taking the flight. A traveler who has placed trust in the airline and its equipment can be said to have faith in them.

When it comes to Jesus, where there is no faith, there is no salvation. He said, "I am the way, and the truth, and the life; no one comes to the Father but through Me" (John 14:6). Just like a traveler must place trust in an airplane and then act on that trust by boarding the airplane in order to arrive at his destination, we must believe the truth about Jesus and then place our trust in Him in order to arrive in heaven when this life has ended.

The trials of Jesus are now a matter of history. Nevertheless, every man and woman since that time has a seat in the jury box. And we, like Pilate, Herod, Pilate's wife, and the angry mob, must reach a verdict within our own hearts. Jesus has presented His case and He has been clear with His answers.

Pilate devalued the truth about the Son of God. Herod was too shallow and vain to see the truth. Pilate's wife accepted everything as truth and so missed seeing it entirely. And the angry mob ignored the truth as inconvenient. What have you done with the truth about the Son of God?

If you would like to learn how to place your trust in Jesus Christ and receive the free gift of eternal life "by grace, through faith," read "How to Begin a Relationship with God" at the end of this book. And if you have questions that have not been answered by what you have read, call or write to Insight for Living using the contact information at the end of this Bible Companion.

Lesson 15

Delivered Up to Be Crucified

<small>MATTHEW 27:27–37 AND JOHN 19:16–30</small>

THE HEART OF THE MATTER

The ancient Roman orator Cicero witnessed the most grisly spectacle of all, crucifiction, and described it as "the most cruel and atrocious of punishments."[1] And although crucifixion was usually reserved for only the most detestable criminals, this was the means by which Jesus died. It would have been a shameful death except that He voluntarily suffered the anguish of crucifixion in order to let guilty people go free. Only as we face the facts of the horrors of His death, can we fully appreciate the price that was paid on Calvary.

DISCOVERING THE WAY

The trials of Jesus came to a predictable end because they arrived at a foregone conclusion. Jesus was not the kind of Messiah the seditious rabble wanted. Jesus was not the puppet ruler the wealthy and powerful could control. Jesus was not the revolutionary threat Pilate hoped he could legitimately condemn. The only matter these divergent factions could agree upon was that the death of Jesus would solve their problems. "So [Pilate] handed Him over to them to be crucified" (John 19:16).

THE CRUELTY OF CRUCIFIXION

By the time of Jesus, civilizations had devised hundreds of ways to kill a man, most of which sought to bring about death as slowly and painfully as possible. The Romans preferred crucifixion because it made the best use of four qualities they prized most in an execution: unrelenting agony, protracted death, public spectacle, and utter humiliation. Barbaric societies especially appreciated the power of humiliation.

 Read Matthew 27:27–44.

What did each group do to humiliate Jesus?
Roman soldiers:

_____

_____

Passers-by:

_____

_____

Chief priests, scribes, and elders:

_____

_____

The robbers:

_____

_____

The Romans didn't invent crucifixion, which dates to the sixth century B.C.,[2] but they turned the technique into a macabre art. An *exactor mortis* was schooled in the finer points of death and led a team of soldiers whose sole task was to make Roman execution a terrifying spectacle. And their experience gave them ample opportunity to experiment with different methods. "Josephus indicated that the soldiers would nail their victims in different positions either for their own amusement or out of rage, sadism, whimsy, or hatred."[3] Over time, they learned how to add various elements to the procedure and adjust them to achieve the desired effect. They could expertly control the amount of suffering, the cause of death, and even when the victim would die.

Before going to the cross, the victim typically endured a scourging, which was accomplished with a *flagrum*, a whip with long, leather tails. The braided leather straps could contain knots or small, metal weights so that the scourging typically resulted in "rib fractures and severe lung bruises and lacerations with bleeding into the chest cavity and partial or complete pneumothorax (collapse of the lung)."[4] This would typically restrict the victim's ability to breathe and send the body into shock. The degree to which the victim was beaten usually determined how long he would survive on the cross. If the executioner wanted the victim to die very quickly, he would choose a *flagrum* with jagged bits of sheep bone braided into the tails.

After the scourging, the victim was forced to carry the implement of his own demise to the place of execution. For Jesus, the path led from the governor's palace out to a remote spot not far from the city wall. A *titulus* inscribed with the victim's crime, was hung around his neck, revealing the reason for his crucifixion to the people he passed along the *via dolorosa*, "the way of suffering."

 Read John 19:16–22.

What "crime" did Pilate write on the *titulus* of Jesus?

_____

_____

Who objected to Pilate's choice of words, and what did they prefer?

_____

_____

Why do you think Pilate was so resolute about the wording?

In Jesus's day, the cross itself was typically made in the shape of a "T", the top crossbeam (the *patibulum*) joined to the vertical member (the *stipes*). Usually, the victim was attached to the cross with his arms outstretched and his feet on the *stipes*, the soles flat against the wood.[5] Hung this way, victims usually took three to five days to die.

To better understand the effects of crucifixion on the body, Dr. Frederick Zugibe, a forensic pathologist, has made crucifixion a topic of scientific study for more than fifty years. His experiments include tying volunteers to a cross in order to observe their behavior and record their physiological response. He closely monitored their respiration, blood pressure, heart rate, circulation, and even the amount of oxygen in their blood. Most people experienced great discomfort within the first half-hour and had to keep their bodies in constant motion to cope with the pain in their arms, chest, back, and legs. The experiments never put the volunteers in danger; nevertheless, the physical stress and fatigue were intense.

Zugibe's experiments, together with his study of historical documents, revealed that death by crucifixion usually came by way of exposure to the elements, dehydration, starvation, or asphyxia. In the case of asphyxia, the victim became too exhausted to pull in another breath and suffocated. If the executioner were especially cruel, he would fit the cross with a *sedile*, a saddle attached about halfway up the cross on which the victim could support his body to temporarily ease his misery, adding days to his crucifixion.

To increase suffering or to hasten the end, the *exactor mortis* could suspend the victim using nails instead of rope, which caused death within hours instead of days. The nail, driven through the palm of the hand close to the wrist, severely damaged the median nerve of the arm and forearm. Within a couple of hours, the victim experienced an affliction known as *causalgia*.

The pain is exquisite and described as an unrelenting, peculiar burning or searing sensation that is so intense that even gentle contacts like clothing or air drafts cause utter torture. It may be aggravated by movement, jarring, noise, or emotion. The pain traverses the arm like lightning bolts. The patient becomes completely preoccupied with avoiding any contact and holding the limb a particular way. . . . Victims of *causalgia* frequently go into shock if the pain is not controlled.[6]

A victim nailed to a cross also had to keep his body in constant motion to relieve the pain in his arms, chest, and legs, which only agitated the damaged nerves in the nail wounds. The primary causes of death were likely hypovolemic shock (excessive blood loss), traumatic shock, or cardiac and respiratory arrest.[7]

Later in John's gospel, the disciple Thomas refers to the imprint of the nails in Jesus's hands (John 20:25–27), so we know Jesus was not merely tied to the cross. Furthermore, the Romans did not want to offend Jewish sensibilities by leaving the three men on their crosses during a very special Sabbath, so they would have chosen the quicker method.

 Read Psalm 22:14–18 and John 19:23–24; 20:25–27.

What striking similarities do you find between David's psalm and the crucifixion of Jesus described in the book of John?

Why did the soldiers choose not to tear Jesus's tunic into pieces? What did they do instead?

Why was this an important event, according to John?

_____

_____

"IT IS FINISHED!"

As evening approached, the religious leaders asked for the legs of the men to be broken in order to hasten death (John 19:31). It is likely that this act prevented the victim from raising up to pull in another breath, thus hastening fatigue asphyxia.[8] The soldiers broke the legs of the other two victims, but when they came to Jesus, he had already died (John 19:32–33).

Jesus deliberately gave up His spirit when His work on the cross was complete (Matthew 27:50; John 19:30). Therefore, the actual cause of His physical death was by His own action. As the Author and Giver of Life, He gave His life away.

Read Matthew 27:16–26.

Who suggested the exchange?

_____

Why do you think he made this suggestion?

_____

_____

For whom was the cross originally intended?

_____

What was Barabbas's crime, according to Luke 23:19?

_____

What was Jesus's crime?

_____

What happened to Barabbas?

Consider the following passages related to the idea of substitution. Then summarize in your own words what you think that concept means.
Leviticus 16:21–22
Isaiah 53:4–6

STARTING YOUR JOURNEY

While Pilate was surprised by the exchange of the innocent for the guilty, no one was more surprised than Barabbas.

Imagine sitting on death row and listening to the trial. Unable to make out Pilate's side of the conversation, all he could hear was the crowd saying:

"Barabbas! . . . Crucify him! Crucify him! Crucify him! . . . His blood shall be upon us and on our children!" (John 19:21, 22–23, 25)

Imagine the panic rising in Barabbas as the guards approached his cell. Imagine his disbelief as his shackles fell to the floor and with a sharp shove from the back, he found himself standing outside. Free.

Scripture doesn't reveal what happened to Barabbas after that day. If you were in his place, how would you have felt?

What would you have done next?

_____

_____

_____

Consider this modern-day illustration.

The man was guilty. No question about it. He stood in the center of the courtroom and offered no rebuttal to the plaintiff's complaint that he hadn't paid his debt. His recent illness had unfortunately resulted in the loss of his job and after paying his medical bills, he couldn't make ends meet.

The judge couldn't disagree. The plaintiff was due his money, the man was indeed guilty of nonpayment, and justice could not be set aside. Nevertheless, the judge's compassion would not allow him to drop the gavel. Not just yet. Once the attorney for the plaintiff had closed his case, the judge suddenly left the courtroom. A few moments later, he returned from his chambers with a check, handed it to the landlord's attorney, and said, "Consider this man's debt paid."

Describe a time you were spared punishment or negative consequences you clearly deserved.

_____

_____

_____

What emotions did you experience as a result?

_____

_____

_____

Who was responsible for sparing you?

Why do you think he or she did this?

There is a name for what you were given. It is called "grace," or unmerited favor.

Grace is free and the highest expression of grace is one that defies explanation. The judge in the previous story displayed extraordinary grace by paying the penalty for another person's debt. This gesture of compassion beautifully illustrates the grace that God has shown us.

We are guilty. No question about it. We have behaved in ways that dishonor God. The commandments of the Old Testament reveal His character and express the values that honor His creation and demonstrate love for Him, but we have broken them. Wrongdoing demands a penalty. The penalty is eternal separation from God in a place of torment, and justice cannot be set aside.

Nevertheless, the compassion of our Judge in heaven has stilled the gavel. "For God so loved the world, that He gave His only begotten Son, that whoever believes in Him shall not perish, but have eternal life" (John 3:16). Jesus, though innocent, took the place of someone who deserved to pay the penalty of death for wrongdoing. He took the place of another on the cross. Yes, Barabbas went free. And the grace he received is merely an illustration of a greater, more personal truth.

You see, it was your place on the cross Jesus took. Jesus died for you.

What if the man in the judge's courtroom had declined his grace, opting for eviction instead? What if Barabbas had said, "Freedom? No, thanks. I'd rather suffer agony on the cross." No one, if he or she understood the nature of eviction or crucifixion, would decline the offer of grace. So, why do people refuse to accept the free gift of eternal life, purchased for them by the death of Jesus Christ in their place?

What has been your response to the offer of grace?

Part 4

The King

(Resurrection)

Lesson 16

Not to Worry . . . He Is Risen!

JOHN 19:32–20:31

THE HEART OF THE MATTER

The Friday before the Jewish Passover Sabbath was a dark day for the followers of Jesus. As their Messiah hung on humankind's most dreadful instrument of death, only John remained at the foot of the cross while the ten remaining disciples scattered and hid themselves. The task of burying Jesus fell to two secret followers who dared to come out of the shadows and a handful of faithful women.

The story of Jesus, however, doesn't end with the cross or even the grave in which He was laid. He is risen! Jesus Christ overcame death and continues to live today. The implications of that astonishing truth are far-reaching, but only for those who choose to believe it. The Gospel accounts tell of four responses to the resurrection of Jesus—the same responses we see today.

DISCOVERING THE WAY

Some skeptics have postulated that Jesus never really died but that He remained in a deep coma until sometime after being placed in the tomb. As anyone who has handled a corpse can testify, entertaining that notion requires more faith than accepting the truth.

PREPARING JESUS'S BODY FOR BURIAL

After the death of Jesus had been confirmed by the centurion's spear and reported to Pilate, two important members of the Jewish ruling council, Joseph of Arimathea and Nicodemus, requested His body (John 19:38–39). These formerly secret disciples and several women would do the gruesome task of preparing His corpse for burial. Once the body of Jesus was lowered from the cross, they would have to flex and massage his arms in order to relieve rigor mortis before bringing them down to His sides. Then they would wash His body and anoint it with balm oil before wrapping it in a single linen cloth. A separate napkin tied under His chin would keep His mouth from gaping open after the muscles began to loosen.

Ordinarily, they would then have wrapped the body tightly from head to toe, using strips of linen soaked in as much as 75 pounds of spiced resin. Then they would have laid Him on a shelf in a tomb excavated from the limestone mountain. After a year had passed and the body had completely decayed, they would have gathered His bones and placed them in a family ossuary—a bone box—along with those of His ancestors.[1] But as the sun sank below the horizon that awful Friday, the burial party found themselves pressed between two of God's commandments. They were to keep the Sabbath day (which began at sundown) sacred by performing no work (Deuteronomy 5:12–15), but they were also required to bury the body of an executed victim on the same day of execution (Deuteronomy 21:22–23). With night closing in, they had just enough time to place Him inside the tomb. The Roman government fixed an official seal over the stone, and the religious leaders posted a guard by the entrance. Joseph, Nicodemus, and the women planned to return the following Sunday morning to complete the task of burial, no doubt under the watchful eye of the temple guard.

 Read Matthew 27:62–66 and 28:1–4.

What did the religious leaders think would happen to the body of Jesus?

_____

_____

Did Pilate seem to share their concern? What was his response?

_____

_____

How did the religious leaders address their concern?

_____

_____

What occurred on Sunday morning to open the tomb?

_____

_____

WITNESSING THE RESURRECTION

The first few hours after this incident were nothing short of pandemonium, of which the four Gospels give account. Very often, when people tell the story of a chaotic event, they include only the details they consider relevant, while leaving out facts they deem to be of secondary importance. They tend to compress some details into summary statements while giving great attention to others. In this case, we have four witnesses to the event, which gives us lots of information.

On the morning after the Sabbath—Sunday morning—Mary Magdalene, another Mary, and some other women converged on the tomb of Jesus. Luke's account reveals that their purpose was to complete the burial process with the spiced resin they had prepared (Luke 24:1). John's record details the experience of Mary Magdalene while Matthew, Mark, and Luke tell us what happened to the other women (Luke 2:10).

As Mary Magdalene and the women approached the tomb, they saw the stone had been moved away from the entrance. According to the Gospel of John, Mary immediately ran to tell Peter and John what had happened (John 20:1–2). Meanwhile, the other women moved in for a closer look.

 Read Matthew 28:1–8.

What did the other women see?

_____

_____

What did they learn about the whereabouts of Jesus?

_____

_____

Do you think they believed that Jesus had risen from the dead? How do you know?

_____

_____

As the women rushed from the tomb, they encountered the risen Jesus, and any doubt they might have had fled away (Matthew 28:9). After assuring them that this would not be the last time they saw Him, Jesus told them to spread the word of His resurrection (Matthew 28:10).

Mary Magdalene, Mary the mother of James, Salome (Mark 16:1), Joanna (Luke 24:10), and an unknown number of other women disciples also encountered the angels and Jesus. The Gospel of John describes Mary Magdalene's experience.

 Read John 20:1–10.

What, specifically, did Mary Magdalene see when she first glimpsed the tomb through the darkness?

_____

_____

What did she assume had happened?

_____

_____

When Peter and John heard the breathless report of Mary Magdalene, they sprinted to the tomb. What did they see?

_____

_____

After studying the Greek terms and phrasing used to describe the empty tomb, Merrill Tenney wrote the following observation:

> There is a strong hint that the clothes were not folded as if Jesus had unwound them and then deposited them in two neat piles on the shelf. The word used to describe the napkin or head cloth does not connote a flat folded square like a table napkin, but a ball of cloth bearing the appearance of being rolled around an object that was no longer there. The wrappings were in position where the body had lain, and the head cloth was where the head had been, separated from the others by the distance from armpits to neck. The shape of the body was still apparent in them, but the flesh and bone had disappeared. . . .
>
> While Peter was cogitating over this puzzle, the other disciple entered the tomb. The account says that "he saw, and believed" ([John] 20:8). The word "saw" (Greek *eidon*) implies mental perception or realization as well as physical sight. In modern language, he "clicked." The answer to the enigma was that Jesus had risen, passing through the graveclothes, which He left undisturbed as a silent proof that death could not hold Him, nor material bonds restrain Him.[2]

Why did the resurrection take Peter and John by surprise (John 20:9)?

_____

_____

When Jesus died, all of the disciples felt hopeless (Luke 24:19–21). How did the perspective of Peter and John change after inspecting the tomb (John 20:8)?

_____

_____

ENCOUNTERING THE RISEN LORD

Once Peter and John left the tomb to tell their respective households that Jesus had risen, Mary Magdalene had an extraordinary encounter of her own. The angels that had greeted the other women appeared to her as well (John 20:11–13). And as she left the garden, she saw the risen Jesus, who gave her the same instructions He gave the other women, "Go find My brothers and tell them" (John 20:14–17 NLT). Luke described what happened when Mary and the other women located the disciples in various places around Jerusalem.

Read Luke 24:8–11.

How did the majority of the disciples regard the report of the women?

_____

_____

Why do you think they had such a hard time believing Jesus had risen?

_____

_____

Later that evening, Jesus's followers gathered in the upper room, perhaps to piece all of the information together to determine what had happened that morning (Luke 24:33–35). As they met, their doubts were put to rest by Jesus's appearance to them (John 20:19–20). However, one disciple had not yet arrived.

 Read John 20:24–25.

Which disciple missed the appearance of Jesus in the upper room?

_____

What was his response to the report of the other followers of Jesus?

_____

_____

Why do you think he struggled to believe the testimony of his trusted friends?

_____

_____

What proof did he demand?

_____

_____

How was his response different from that of the other disciples when Jesus appeared in Luke 24:36–40?

_____

_____

Eight days later, the followers of Jesus were still coming to terms with what had happened. Even after seeing the risen Jesus with their own eyes, "they still could not believe it because of their joy and amazement" (Luke 24:41). Eventually, those who doubted received the proof they needed and they believed as well. Yet many witnesses to the events of that Sunday morning never believed.

Review Matthew 27:62–66 and 28:11–15.

To whom did the detachment of guards report after witnessing the earthquake and the opening of the tomb?

_____

_____

How did they respond after hearing the guards' report?

_____

_____

How was their response to the resurrection different from that of Thomas and the other disciples?

_____

_____

_____

_____

STARTING YOUR JOURNEY

The responses of the people impacted by the resurrection of Jesus generally fall into one of four categories:

Some believed immediately. They were given the information, remembered what Jesus had predicted several times during his ministry, put all of the facts together, and accepted His resurrection as genuine.

Some believed with indirect evidence. They initially doubted the notion, but when they received further information, such as seeing an empty tomb, they knew He had risen.

Some believed with direct evidence. They only believed that Jesus had risen after seeing Him with their own eyes.

Some never believed. They had all the evidence they needed to confirm that His resurrection was genuine, but refused to acknowledge or accept the truth.

For each of the people listed below, describe his or her response to the events and why you think he or she reacted this way.

Mary Magdalene

_____

_____

The "other women" (Mary the mother of James, Salome, Joanna, etc.)

_____

_____

Peter

_____

_____

John

_____

_____

The majority of Jesus's followers

_____

_____

Thomas

_____

_____

The guards

_____

_____

The religious leaders

_____

_____

People generally tend to respond to the news of Jesus's resurrection the same today as they did that surprising Sunday morning. Some believe almost immediately. Many want to examine the evidence. Others must have personal experience with the supernatural—real or imagined—before they will believe. And a great many refuse to accept His resurrection as genuine, regardless.

Which category best describes your response to the claim that Jesus rose from the dead? Why?

_____

_____

_____

Think of someone you know who is skeptical of Jesus's resurrection. Of the responses listed above, which best describes the reaction of this person?

_____

_____

_____

The pages of history are filled with the stories of great people. While these great lives continue to make us better by their legacy, none was so great as to overcome death. Only one continues to live and has the power to offer us His kind of life: life after death.

The next lesson examines the implications of the resurrection for the followers of Jesus.

Lesson 17

Encountering Jesus along Life's Road

THE HEART OF THE MATTER

Fantastic! Outstanding! Incredible! Thanks to blockbuster movies, thrill rides, and Madison Avenue ad campaigns, we have come to expect that if life isn't "sensational," something must be wrong. If we are not careful, we can apply those expectations to our spiritual journey and fail to see the hand of God in the ordinary events of life. Even more tragic, we might fail to recognize His loving care for us in the midst of trials.

Let's face it, life typically isn't fantastic. Usually, life is ordinary and sometimes painful. But that is when we do the most learning and growing. That is when we have the greatest opportunity to encounter the risen Jesus . . . if we have eyes to see.

DISCOVERING THE WAY

Prior to His arrest, Jesus traveled up and down the strip of land once ruled by David and Solomon, inviting the people of Israel to become a part of His kingdom, promising abundant life. His followers fully expected that He would become their king and that Israel would again be prosperous and free. He was their Messiah. But on one fateful Friday afternoon, as the sun fell behind the horizon, the Son of God hung cold and lifeless on a Roman cross just outside the city walls.

As the sun rose on Sunday morning and the Passover feast came to an end, two of Jesus's followers, disillusioned and resolving to leave their foolish dreams in Jerusalem forever, left for home. The dejected pair began the seven-mile walk to Emmaus even as rumors of resurrection circulated among the ranks of Jesus's disciples (Luke 24:13).

 Read Luke 24:13–17.

What were the two followers doing when Jesus approached them?

_____

_____

Why were they unable to recognize Jesus? (See also Mark 16:12.)

_____

_____

Why do you think Jesus chose to approach them this way?

_____

_____

Luke describes the disciples' conversation as bantering ideas back and forth with great emotion in a shared search for answers (Luke 24:14–16). The Greek phrase *homileo suzeteo*, "talking and discussing" (24:15), would be more literally translated as "conversing"[1] and "disputing."[2] The disillusioned followers desperately wanted to know why their expectations of the Messiah had come to such a tragic end.

AN ENLIGHTENING CONVERSATION

 Read Luke 24:18–24.

Luke employed a clever narrative device called literary irony, in which the reader is aware of important facts that are hidden from the characters. Jesus asked a question designed to engage the men in conversation, but Cleopas' reply reveals a delightful paradox for the reader: "Are You the only one visiting Jerusalem and unaware of the things which have happened here in these days?" (Luke 24:18) Of course, if anyone understood what had happened, it was Jesus! The two men continued on, describing the events of recent days.

Cleopas and his companion "stood still, looking sad" (24:17). Following the narrative in Luke 24:19–24, describe, as best you can, their perspective on Jesus's death and resurrection.

_____

_____

_____

_____

_____

How does your perspective as the reader differ from theirs?

_____

_____

_____

Describe your feelings toward the two as you observe their confusion and sadness.

_____

_____

_____

_____

_____

They did not believe Jesus had risen from the dead, so they were left with three faulty perspectives.

First, *their viewpoint lacked a spiritual dimension, leaving them with a human understanding of the events.*

According to Cleopas, what caused Jesus's death? (See Luke 24:19–20 once again.)

_____

_____

Read Peter's perspective in Acts 2:22–23; 3:18; and 4:27–28. What does he say brought about Jesus's suffering and death?

_____

_____

Second, *their own agenda determined their expectations.*

Read Luke 24:21. What did Cleopas expect the Messiah to do?

_____

_____

Try to put yourself in his shoes. If you had followed Jesus and experienced the same things Cleopas did, how would you have felt?

_____

Many disciples made the mistake of thinking that the Messiah would merely recapture the glory days of King David. In other words, they hoped Jesus would bring Israel the same power and prosperity she once enjoyed, only magnified and multiplied. Given their exclusive worship of God, this would not be an inappropriate wish. But compared to the reality that lay before them—Roman oppression and a dead Messiah—their hopes for glory seemed to have been utterly destroyed.

Third, *they failed to acknowledge the resurrection.*

Choose a few of the following passages to read:

Matthew 16:21 (Mark 8:31; Luke 9:22)
Matthew 17:22–23 (Mark 9:31; Luke 9:44)
Matthew 20:18–19 (Mark 10:33–34; Luke 18:32–33)
Mark 14:27–28
John 2:18–21

In your own words, summarize the events Jesus predicted would occur.

_____

_____

_____

_____

Now read Luke 24:21–24. What evidence supports the conclusion that Jesus had risen from the dead? What do you think Cleopas and his companion thought of this evidence?

_____

_____

_____

_____

If these two followers believed that Jesus had risen from the dead, two things would have been true. First, they would have been walking *toward* Jerusalem to see the risen Lord, not away. Second, they would have seen the trials, crucifixion, and burial of Jesus as the fulfillment of all He promised, not as the end of their hopes.

Read Luke 24:25–27.
The Gospel accounts of Jesus's life were originally documents intended to be read aloud in Christian gatherings. When the reader reached the part of the story in which Cleopas recounted the events of the past three

days, the tension among the listeners must have been unbearable, because the two followers simply did not have the eyes to see what should have been plainly visible (Luke 24:16).

ENCOUNTERED BY TRUTH

Finally, Jesus broke His silence to bring a reproof, ask a question, and offer an explanation. In the reproof, "O foolish men and slow of heart to believe in all that the prophets have spoken!" (Luke 24:25), Jesus demonstrated that the two followers knew the contents of Scripture but did not accept its message as truth. As a result, they failed to see God's sovereign plan. His question, "Was it not necessary for the Christ to suffer these things and to enter into His glory?" pointed to the reason for their unbelief (Luke 24:26). They had confused their own expectations with the hope God was offering, and they had failed to see God's ultimate purpose.

To help the two followers see, Jesus reviewed the entire history of Israel from the time of the Exodus to His own resurrection, highlighting God's plan for the Messiah (24:27).[3]

DIGGING DEEPER

The Suffering Servant

The prophetic book of Isaiah features a series of "Servant Songs" that punctuate the latter half of the prophet's oracle to the nation of Israel. These songs feature the mission of "the Servant of the Lord"— bringing justice to the world (Isaiah 42:1–4), leading His people into a right relationship with God (49:5), enlightening the nations and bringing salvation to everyone (49:6), enduring unjust humiliation (50:6), and bearing the divine punishment others deserve (52:13–53:12).

The final song applauds the Servant for His sacrifice and extols His path to glory through His own humiliation. In the Old Testament, God established the practice of animal sacrifice to cover the sins of His people. In the case of the Servant, unlike the Hebrew sacrifice in which *one* lamb was received by God as a token for *one* person's sin, "the Lord has caused the iniquity of *us all* to fall on Him [the Servant]" (Isaiah 53:6).

Isaiah's final "Servant Song" promised something so much greater to the Jewish nation than liberation from the burden of Roman occupation. It foretold the Messiah's real purpose on Earth—liberation from the burden of sin's penalty, which was death (Isaiah 53:5–6).

Read Luke 24:28–35.

In keeping with ancient Near-Eastern rules of hospitality, the two followers then invited the "stranger" to stay the night. Jesus accepted their offer, yet maintained His cover in order to complete the lesson He had begun teaching them just outside Jerusalem (Luke 24:28–29).

What caused the men to finally recognize the stranger as Jesus (see 24:40)?

_____

_____

The Greek phrase *ophthalmos dianoigo epiginosko*, translated "eyes were opened and they recognized Him," literally means "their eyes were *completely* opened"[4] and "they came to *fully comprehend* Him."[5] This action was more than a mere recognition of His features. They came to recognize Jesus in all His significance as the Messiah, the Suffering Servant, the Son of God, and their risen Lord! Then Jesus literally became "invisible"—*aphantos*—meaning that He suddenly vanished from their midst once their eyes were open.[6]

Compare Luke 24:17, 19–24 with 24:32–35. Based on the behavior of Cleopas and his companion, describe the transformation in their thinking.

_____

According to 24:16, their eyes were prevented from recognizing Jesus. He revealed His identity only after taking great pains to explain to them "the things concerning Himself in all the Scriptures." Why do you think He took this approach rather than revealing His identity from the start?

_____

Do you think the transformation in their thinking would have been as effective if Jesus had revealed his identity first? Explain your answer.

_____

Luke concludes this story with another bit of irony. The disciples had been staring into the face of the risen Jesus, yet they were prevented from seeing him until they buried their faulty expectations. Then, a careful review of the Scriptures gave them a divine perspective on what they once saw as dismal circumstances. Once their eyes were opened to the reality and implications of the resurrection, Jesus became visible to their physical eyes. Now, their new, resurrected hope carried them back to Jerusalem to bear the good news to others (Luke 24:33–35).

STARTING YOUR JOURNEY

As Luke tells the story of the two despondent disciples on the road to Emmaus, we cannot help but identify with their pain.

We, too, are pilgrims on a journey through life. We, too, despair of life's circumstances from time to time. We, too, lose heart when our expectations come to a tragic end. But remember, every trial is an opportunity to discover what God wants us to see.

What expectations do you now maintain that are causing you the most disappointment, discouragement, or frustration?

_____

_____

_____

_____

How has this affected your understanding of God's purpose and plan?

_____

_____

_____

As in the case of the two followers on the road to Emmaus, we must allow God to open our eyes. While this is something He must do on our behalf, we can nonetheless make the process less difficult in four specific ways.

1. Invite God in.

Have you invited the Lord into your life? Cleopas and his companion listened intently to the Voice of truth and invited Him into their home. If you haven't begun a relationship with God, you will continue to struggle in vain. For more information, see "How to Begin a Relationship with God" in the back of this Bible Companion.

2. Surrender your expectations.

Personalize the following prayer and then offer it to God.

My Heavenly Father,
    I greatly desire _____ .
**While this expectation is mostly honorable and good, it is nonethe-
less mine and may not be Yours. I am frustrated and disillusioned
because all my efforts to accomplish what I believe to be right fail
to accomplish anything. Therefore, I must accept that the outcome
I desire is not what You desire.**
    **Lord, I release my expectation, and I humbly ask You to accom-
plish Your will in whatever manner You see fit and in whatever time
You consider appropriate.**

Amen.

3. Seek God's perspective.

To help the two disciples see their circumstances from God's perspective, Jesus explained the Scriptures. And we have the same opportunity to
share God's vantage point by reading our only completely reliable source
of truth, the sixty-six books of the Bible. This doesn't have to be complicated. Simply set aside as little as ten minutes each day, start at the Book
of Genesis, and read.

4. Trust God's timing.

God, in His perfect discernment, did not allow the two disciples to
recognize Jesus until the time was right. He didn't allow them to suffer in
grief a moment longer than was absolutely necessary, yet He didn't end
their discomfort too soon. Spiritual maturity rarely occurs instantaneously.
Growth usually requires a journey and journeys take time. Submit to God's
will and trust His timing. He is faithful.

**When you're tempted to return to the expectation you gave to the
Lord in prayer—and you will be—how can you remind yourself to
release it once again? Brainstorm at least two practical reminders.**

Circumstances, especially those involving loss, are usually perceived as difficult because reality does not mesh with our expectations. The two followers on the road to Emmaus undoubtedly felt utterly alone as they mourned the death of their dreams. During their suffering, God was indeed nearby, and He allowed their pain to continue until their own desires no longer held them captive.

Like the two on the road to Emmaus, you do not travel alone. God is with you. Are you willing to see Him?

Lesson 18

Listening to Jesus beside the Sea

JOHN 21:1–22

THE HEART OF THE MATTER

We can learn a lot about our relationship with God by studying the life of Peter. His journey with Jesus is a study in contradictions. In the midst of a raging storm, he impulsively climbed out of his boat at the invitation of Jesus to walk on water, only to divert his attention and sink like a stone (Matthew 14:28–30). His affirmation, "You are the Christ, the Son of the living God," brought him high praise and the prediction he would someday lead the church (16:13–19), but from that great height, he soon fell to receive a sharp rebuke (16:21–23). Then, after risking his life to defend his Master against a cohort of soldiers, he denied knowing Jesus to the rabble huddled in the courtyard at His trial (John 18:10, 17, 25–27).

But, after Jesus's death and resurrection, a seaside reunion with the risen Lord changed everything. Peter learned that being a disciple requires one primary qualification: a willingness to follow.

DISCOVERING THE WAY

Simon's brother, Andrew, had been a follower of John the Baptizer for some time when he first encountered Jesus. After witnessing the remarkable events surrounding Jesus's baptism,

Andrew took his brother to the man they would come to know as the Messiah (John 1:35–41). Soon after meeting Simon, Jesus gave him the name Peter (*Cephas* in Aramaic, *Petros* in Greek), which means "rock" (John 1:42).

FISHERS OF MEN

Sometime later, perhaps after weeks or even months of interaction, Peter and his business associates were cleaning their nets by the Sea of Galilee after a long night of fishing. As they carried out the task, Jesus used Peter's boat as a speaking platform (Luke 5:1–3).

 Read Luke 5:4–7.

Why did Simon initially object to Jesus's request?

Why do you think he ultimately agreed to go, though it was against his own best judgment?

What was the result of his obedience?

Read Luke 5:8–11.

Peter's reaction to the miracle of Jesus was similar to several Old Testament encounters (Exodus 20:19; 33:20; Judges 13:22; Job 42:5–6; Isaiah 6:5). When the simple fisherman recognized the divine power of Jesus, knowledge of his own sinfulness brought him to his knees, trembling with fear (Luke 5:8).

Jesus responded to Peter's act of worship and submission with two phrases: a reassurance and a call. Write them in your own words.

What did Peter do in response to Jesus's call?

Peter had never been accused of being overly humble. In fact, throughout the Gospel accounts of Jesus's ministry, he was frequently brash, quick to blurt out what others merely thought, impulsive, and let his emotions propel him through life. This was likely true of the moment he decided to drop his fishing nets and follow Jesus, who, of course, knew his character better than anyone.

"I Don't Know Him"

On the eve of His arrest and trials, Jesus gathered His disciples for a final meal together. In the solitude of a private dining room, He gave them His final instructions.

 Read John 13:34–38.

Did Peter consider himself to be a committed disciple of Jesus? What evidence did he give to prove his dedication? (Note the comparison he makes in Matthew 26:31–35 and Mark 14:27–31.)

Though Peter's confidence may appear to be little more than bravado, he initially backed up his boast with bold action. Lopping off the ear of one of the men who came to arrest Jesus, he would have taken on a whole contingent of warriors with little more than a kitchen knife (John 18:10).

Later that evening, Peter warmed himself over a fire as the first trial of Jesus drew to a close. A relative of the man Peter had injured stood nearby, recognized him, and asked, "Did I not see you in the garden with Him [Jesus]?" (John 18:26). Peter's vehement protest marked his third denial of Jesus that evening (18:27). Just then, as a rooster crowed in the distance, the door to the court chamber opened and Peter, gazing across the glowing embers of the fire, caught his Master's eyes. Suddenly the weight of disappointment crushed the life out of him and he wept bitterly (Luke 22:60–62).

Shortly thereafter, a squad of executioners led Jesus to the outskirts of Jerusalem, stretched out His arms, and slowly killed Him. Three days later, He left the grave and began appearing to His many followers, including Peter and the other disciples. But after the flush of excitement had passed, an obvious question arose among the twelve who had left everything and followed Jesus—"*What now?*"

FOLLOW ME

Peter, perhaps convinced that his failure had disqualified him from leadership, returned to the familiarity of his fishing boat, where at least he had a rudder to steer him through the tempest and where an honest day's labor earned a decent catch of fish. Fishing for men required more dedication than he could promise anymore.

As the blue-grey twilight turned pink on the horizon and the prime time for fishing passed, Peter and his crew steered the boat toward the shore. Soon, however, his life would take a very different course.

 Read John 21:1–8.

As you compare the scene in John 21:1–6 with Luke 5:1–6, what similarities do you see?

_____

_____

What did Peter do when he heard that the man on the shore was Jesus? What do you think this says about Peter's personality?

_____

_____

What principle do you think Jesus was trying to illustrate by giving the disciples such a large load of fish?

_____

_____

Translate this principle into your own life. What does it mean to you, in a practical sense?

_____

_____

As the other disciples made it to shore, Jesus had a fire burning with His own supply of fish cooking over the flame. He invited His pupils to add their fish to His as He finished preparing their breakfast. After breaking the bread and dividing the cooked fish among them, Jesus sat by the fire and enjoyed the company of His friends (John 21:9–14).

As the other men listened in, Jesus gazed across the fire and put a difficult question before His impulsive student, Peter.

GETTING TO THE ROOT
The Three Loves

The Greek language has at least three words for *love*. When Greeks thought of the love between a man and a woman, they used the word *eros*. It describes the euphoric, "in-love" feelings that cause sparks to fly early in a romance. *Philos* describes the warm affection shared by friends, close family members, and even romantic lovers. The verb form, *phileo*, means, "to treat somebody as one of one's own people."[1] The

Greeks held *philos* in high regard as a deeply emotional connection between people.

A third word, *agape*, in contrast to *eros*, is anything but impetuous. And, whereas *philos* describes affection, *agape* speaks of commitment: "Here is a love that makes distinctions, choosing its objects freely. Hence it is especially the love of a higher for a lower. It is active, not self-seeking love."[2] *Agape* loves God first, loves neighbor as self, and loves enemies and friends alike. It forgives faults and finds its highest expression when it is least deserved.

Read John 21:15–19.

When Jesus asked Peter, "Do you love me?" He used the verb *agapao* the first two times. To these questions Peter responded using the word *phileo*. Of his own affection, Peter could be sure. As to commitment, his failure had left him with grave doubts. On the third inquiry, Jesus adopted Peter's word choice, as if to accept the humbled disciple's timidity.

Why do you think Jesus included a comparison with the other disciples in His first question?

_____

_____

_____

What command did Jesus issue after each of Peter's tentative responses?

_____

_____

_____

Jesus indicated that Peter's discipleship would eventually cost him his life. What kind of death did Jesus describe?

What might Peter have thought when he heard Jesus's prediction?

We naturally expect that the person most qualified to be a leader is the man or woman who has the greatest natural ability and accomplishments. A significant failure usually means termination or demotion. That's the way the world works. But not the Kingdom of God. The chief duty of a spiritual leader is to follow Jesus!

After Peter's dismal failure in the courtyard, humility displaced his bravado. Jesus took His emptied, forlorn disciple back to the beginning. With a huge haul of fish flopping in the background, the result of obedience to the word of Jesus, Peter heard—perhaps for the first time clearly—the simple call of his Master: "Follow Me" (John 21:19).

 Read John 21:20–23.

Why do you think Peter concerned himself with the Lord's plan for John's life?

How did Jesus respond to Peter's comparison?

The last recorded words of Jesus in the Gospel of John appear especially emphatic in Greek. Literally translated, Jesus said to Peter, "You . . . Me . . . keep following."

STARTING YOUR JOURNEY

Peter's personality resonates especially well in our democratic, entrepreneurial, self-determined culture. We cheer those who desire more power and wealth and those who inspire others with their infectious desire to conquer new territory or overcome daunting challenges. Those are the people we love to follow.

Leadership from the perspective of God is very different. Only one quality is required: a willingness to follow Jesus Christ. He has said to you, "You . . . Me . . . keep following." Your calling is unique because your journey will be unlike anyone else's. Though it will affect others, it applies only to you. It is both costly and rewarding. It will likely lead you to places that frighten you now but will feel as natural as home when the time is right. Your only responsibility is the same as the only requirement of discipleship: obedience to the call. Follow Him!

As you examine the specific calling of Jesus Christ on your life, consider three important lessons from the call of Peter in John 21:1–23.

1. When the Lord offers an opportunity to change futility into fruitfulness, be open to change.

What are you pursuing that continually ends in futility?

Why do you continue to pursue this goal, hope, or expectation? Be honest.

Have you sensed the Lord offering you an opportunity to let this go? If so, why are you still holding on?

_____

_____

_____

Has He made you aware of an opportunity to exchange it for something positive, something that will result in godly fruit in your life or in the lives of others? What is it? What is the first step you need to take in order to begin?

_____

_____

_____

Be careful to avoid interpreting circumstances as indicators of God's will. Note that Jesus called Peter to leave his profession as a fisherman— a significant change in direction—*even after giving him a miraculously large catch.* The Lord never hides His will from us. The difficulty lies in keeping other concerns from diverting our attention.

2. When He plans to move you in a new and challenging direction, expect a period of deep soul-searching.

Finding clarity can be a difficult challenge when distractions clamor for your attention. The days following the resurrection of Jesus were probably quiet ones for Peter, and he likely felt cast aside. But when the time was right, Jesus confronted His formerly impetuous disciple with a challenge. For Peter, the defining issue was love. Whom did he love and would honoring that love be his first priority? Once those questions had been answered, his future became clear.

As you review your calendar and your checkbook, do a little soul-searching. What do they indicate is your first priority? What does that say about your spiritual life?

_____

_____

How can you rearrange your financial and time commitments to make following the Lord your first priority?

_____

_____

How do these actions indicate or facilitate a willingness to follow God?

_____

_____

3. When He makes it clear that you are to follow Him in this new direction, focus fully on Him and refuse to be distracted by comparisons with others.

Does the faithfulness of other people encourage you to follow Christ, or does it leave you feeling inadequate? Explain your answer.

_____

_____

_____

Beware the power of comparisons! Even as Peter heard the call of Jesus for the fourth time, he could not resist a glance over his shoulder. John was the only disciple who had remained with Jesus throughout His ordeal. Jesus had even entrusted him with the care of His mother (John 19:26–27). Peter must have thought, *Who am I compared to Mr. Faithfulness?* But Jesus clarified the issue. John was responsible for John. Peter was responsible for Peter. And each had only one command to heed: "Follow Me."

If anyone had disqualified himself as the leader of the Christians, it was certainly the one who denied his relationship with Jesus when the situation grew tense. Who would want an emotional, vacillating, firebrand to lead the people of God? Jesus did. After Peter came to recognize his own inadequacy apart from Christ, he became a rock-solid leader. As his story unfolds in the book of Acts, we can clearly see that when Peter fixed his eyes on Jesus and followed Him, others followed too. And they followed by the thousands.

Lesson 19

Challenged by Jesus on the Mountain

MATTHEW 28:16–20; MARK 16:14–16; AND ACTS 1:6–8

THE HEART OF THE MATTER

Jesus did something marvelous when He became a man and when He redeemed humanity from the death-grip of sin. Through His death, burial, and resurrection, we are able to receive life. He also did something marvelous when He gave His followers the task of carrying the message of salvation to all humankind. He could have done this Himself, but He called His followers to join Him in His victory over sin and evil.

Forty days after His resurrection, Jesus called the eleven disciples and a host of followers to a mountaintop in Galilee to deliver what we now call the "Great Commission." In this mandate, He revealed the part all Christians are to play in bringing the message of eternal salvation to the world.

DISCOVERING THE WAY

After His resurrection, Jesus appeared to His followers on numerous occasions to offer hope, to forgive failures, to give counsel, and to leave final instructions. After forty days of regular interaction, He summoned His followers for a crucial personal encounter. At that time, He would answer the one question troubling every mind: *What now?*

THE GREAT COMMISSION

Read Matthew 28:16–20.

Matthew reveals that Jesus directly charged His inner circle of eleven disciples to meet Him in Galilee, but several clues in Scripture suggest that He also expected to address a multitude of followers. The phrase "some were doubtful" (Matthew 28:17) would not accurately describe the eleven disciples who had seen Him so many times and who already believed in His resurrection. More likely, this description refers to other followers who had not yet seen Jesus after His resurrection. Furthermore, Paul's description of His appearance to "more than five hundred brethren at one time" (1 Corinthians 15:6) may be this very encounter, the content of which would explain why Jesus chose such a large venue for this vitally important assembly.

Jesus gathered His followers in order to charge them with the important mission of sharing the gospel. Whenever someone in a higher position delegates a task to another, their interaction involves three primary issues: responsibility, authority, and accountability.

Responsibility defines the assignment, which must be clear and specific to both parties. For example, if a supervisor sends an employee to purchase office supplies, the employee needs to know exactly what to buy. He or she needs a list.

Authority establishes the empowerment to carry out the assignment. The employee charged with purchasing office supplies must be given sufficient money to cover the cost. And if a colleague challenges the employee, he or she must be able to say, "I'm doing what the boss instructed me to do."

Having received a responsibility and the authority to carry it out, the employee owes his or her boss *accountability.* The employee charged with purchasing office supplies must answer for his or her use of the money and return with the supplies.

The words of Jesus in the Great Commission have been reproduced in the sentence diagram that follows. Take a few moments to study the relationships between the words and clauses, and then answer the questions.

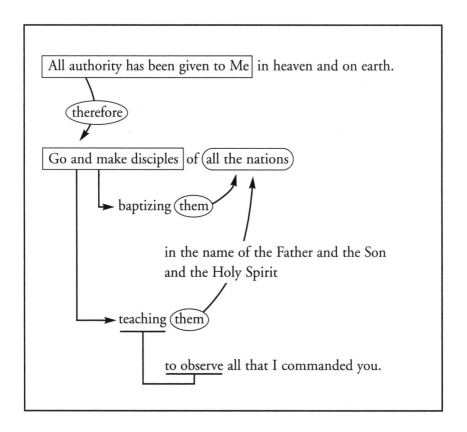

All authority has been given to Me in heaven and on earth.

therefore

Go and make disciples of all the nations

baptizing them

in the name of the Father and the Son and the Holy Spirit

teaching them

to observe all that I commanded you.

What primary responsibility did Jesus delegate to His followers in the first part of Matthew 28:19?

Read Romans 5:8 and 10:9–10. How does someone become a disciple of Jesus Christ?

Now read Romans 10:14–15. Briefly summarize these verses in your own words. What then is your role in making disciples?

_____

_____

_____

Look back at the diagram of Matthew 28:19–20. Jesus used two "-ing" verbs to indicate the steps in making disciples. What are they?

_____

_____

_____

DIGGING DEEPER

The Purpose of Baptism

Teaching others to follow Jesus's commands is generally not all that controversial. But the idea of baptism has traditionally been a point of contention among some Christians. Some teach that small children should be baptized as a means of dedication to Jesus. Others advocate that baptism should only be performed as a way to show the community that an individual has trusted Christ for his or her salvation. And still others teach that you must be baptized to receive eternal life.

The Bible is clear about the relationship between baptism and trusting Christ—*first* you must trust Christ in faith, and *then* you should be baptized. When Peter preached to the multitude, thousands believed his words about the death and resurrection of Jesus and were then baptized (Acts 2:6). When Philip spoke with the Ethiopian eunuch about Jesus, the man said, "I believe that Jesus Christ is the Son of God." Philip stopped the chariot and baptized him (Acts 8:37–38). Baptism is *not* a requirement for salvation. Salvation comes only by grace, through faith in Jesus Christ. Baptism is an act of obedience that follows a person's decision to trust Christ, and it publicly declares his or her commitment as His disciple.

MAKE DISCIPLES

The main verb phrase in Matthew 28:19 is "make disciples." It isn't "go," and it isn't "baptize." It isn't even "teach." All of those verbs are subordinate to the main verb. So the goal of the Great Commission is not just winning souls. It is reaching them with the gospel and staying with them as they become learners, growing in the faith.

Is "making a disciple" something that can be done quickly or easily? Explain your answer.

GETTING TO THE ROOT
Disciples on the "Go"

The Greek word *poreuō*, translated as "go" in the Great Commission, is a participle ("going").[1] Some preachers and teachers suggest that Jesus's command should be rendered, "while you are going, make disciples," implying that evangelism doesn't have to include anything beyond a natural part of our daily routine. While the Lord would certainly agree that making disciples is not just the responsibility of missionaries and that all believers should be looking for opportunities to share the good news with others, this is not how a reader in His day would interpret this command.

The phrase "go and make disciples" uses the participle in the same manner the angel did in warning Joseph, the step-father of Jesus: "Get up! Take the Child . . ." (Matthew 2:13). The angel did not say to Joseph, "While you are getting up, take the Child . . . ." Herod's intention to kill the Christ Child demanded urgency.

Both "go" and "get up" are what Greek scholars call an "attendant circumstance participle."[2] When a participle is used in this manner, it adopts the character of the main verb to which it is attached; in this case, "make disciples."

The command of Jesus is both clear and urgent: "Go, make disciples." This command is not just for the paid professionals—missionaries and preachers. All Christians should take part in fulfilling it.

WITNESSES IN JERUSALEM, JUDEA, SAMARIA, AND THE WORLD

Read Acts 1:6–8.

In Acts 1, Luke introduced his history of the church and the beginnings of Christianity with Jesus's final words to the church. Having spent forty days instructing His followers "concerning the kingdom of God" (Acts 1:3), Jesus promised the imminent arrival of the Holy Spirit. However, just like the two men on the road to Emmaus (Luke 24:13–35), these disciples wondered about the restoration of Israel with Jesus ruling in power (Acts 1:6).

Did Jesus refute or correct the disciples' expectations concerning the future of Israel? _____

What does His answer suggest will eventually occur?

_____

_____

What is the first word in Acts 1:8? _____

What does this indicate about Jesus's intention regarding the disciples' focus? (Hint: See Acts 1:6.)

_____

_____

What two predictions did Jesus make in Acts 1:8?

You will _____

You shall _____

What geographical place did Jesus list first, indicating this was where evangelism would begin for the disciples?

_____

In what region did Jesus say evangelism should occur next?

_____

Where did Jesus say evangelism should extend in due course?

_____

The epicenter of evangelism was Jerusalem, the birthplace of the church. Jesus's disciples were to be witnesses for Christ first to their family, friends, neighbors, and coworkers. "Judea" referred to the area surrounding Jerusalem, in what we might call a city, county, or state. "Samaria" indicated the neighboring region in which relations would be cross-cultural—telling others of different faiths and races about Jesus Christ. Finally, they were to carry the good news to all parts of the world.

Read Acts 1:9–11.

Where did Jesus go after instructing His followers?

_____

What did the angels say would occur sometime in the future?

_____

What do their words imply that the followers of Jesus, including us, should do in the meantime?

_____

_____

STARTING YOUR JOURNEY

A study of Matthew 28:16–20 and Acts 1:3–11 yields no less than four observations that encourage and inspire us to apply the Great Commission in our everyday lives.

First, *Jesus spoke to very ordinary people who knew Him personally.*

The eleven disciples and Jesus's other followers couldn't claim any special knowledge. They didn't occupy special positions of power or privilege. They weren't especially "spiritual," and they had no special status as "clergy." Most were fishermen, tax collectors, or day laborers whose only distinction was their decision to follow Jesus. Nevertheless, Jesus called them to earnestly engage in carrying the good news of salvation to every part of the world.

In what way does the Great Commission involve you?

_____

_____

_____

_____

Do you feel adequate to take part in Jesus's instructions? Why, or why not? If not, what keeps you from sharing Christ with those around you?

_____

_____

_____

_____

Second, *Jesus presented the game plan clearly and simply.*

What is the objective of the Great Commission? It's to go, make disciples by baptizing them and teaching them (Matthew 28:19). It's that simple. You don't have to know Greek. You don't have to be super-spiritual. You just have to be willing to reach people with the gospel and to stay with them as they learn.

As one of Christ's followers, you have been given the responsibility of the Great Commission. In your own words, explain the instructions that Jesus gave in Matthew 28:19–20, personalizing each part.

_____

_____

_____

Brainstorm two or three examples of how you might carry out this command in your everyday life.

_____

_____

_____

Third, *Jesus was intense about the mission but relaxed regarding the method.*

Go back and look at Matthew 28:19 again. Jesus's command is clear: "Make disciples." But notice what He didn't say. Aside from baptizing and teaching, He didn't prescribe a method for disciple-making. Why? Because they vary just as people do. Jesus wants us to focus on the mission of making disciples, but He gives us freedom to be creative in how we go about it.

Describe a method of sharing the gospel that you have seen in action and found to be particularly effective.

_____

_____

Describe a method of sharing the gospel that you have found to be ineffective or even counterproductive.

_____

_____

Finally, *the "Great Commission" requires action.*

Which individual, group of people, or culture do you feel most compelled to approach with the good news of Jesus Christ?

_____

_____

How can you engage the help of others as you "go and make disciples"?

_____

_____

While God certainly does not need our help to reach and teach the world, He has nevertheless chosen to include us in His plan. The Old Testament prophets and the book of Revelation unambiguously point to the victory of good over evil. Sin and death will eventually succumb to the unstoppable power of Jesus Christ (Isaiah 25:8; Revelation 21:3–4). Therefore, the Great Commission is essentially an invitation to join God in a great enterprise that has no chance of failure. He does not need us, but He does want us.

Have you responded to His invitation?

Lesson 20

Watching for Jesus in the Air

1 Corinthians 15:50–57; 1 Thessalonians 4:13–18;
Titus 2:11–13

THE HEART OF THE MATTER

The world, created and deemed good by God, no longer operates according to His rules. Because sin entered the world through the disobedience of humankind, there's something wrong with everything. But all is not lost. God sent His Son, Jesus Christ, for the purpose of redeeming His creation, including humanity. Jesus paid the penalty for our sin on the cross, has commissioned His followers to make disciples of all people, and will appear in the clouds at any moment for His church. When He comes, those who died as believers in Jesus Christ will rise from the dead, believers who are alive will be transformed, and we all will ascend to meet Him in the sky. Then, at God's appointed time, Jesus will come a second time to earth and establish His kingdom.

He could come at any moment. Are you prepared to meet Him face to face?

DISCOVERING THE WAY

The world was not always the twisted, sin-filled place it is now. "In the beginning, God created the heavens and the earth," (Genesis 1:1), filled the universe with truth, gave it order, and called it "good" (Genesis 1:31). Note that the Lord declared His creation to be "good" no less than seven times in the creation account (see Genesis 1:4, 10, 12, 18, 21, 25, 31). But then came a tragedy of monumental proportions. The first man and woman disobeyed this simple command of God:

> "From any tree of the garden you may eat freely; but from the tree of the knowledge of good and evil you shall not eat, for in the day that you eat from it you will surely die." (Genesis 2:16–17)

Adam and Eve's willful disobedience changed *everything.* Theologians refer to this event as "the Fall," for in that moment sin began its cascading corruption of the world, transforming it from the good God had created into a menacing perversion (Genesis 3:14–24). The earth now produces crops hampered by weeds and thorns. Work has become grinding toil. The joy of childbirth comes at the expense of enormous pain and anguish. Our very nature as people—created to bear the image of God—has been distorted by sin. Even the good we do is often laced with selfishness or impure motives. And sin brought with it the ultimate affront to God: death, and the decay and termination of everything He created to be good.

God didn't become human in the person of Jesus merely to offset our evil with His good. The ways of earth and heaven are entirely incompatible. No, the birth of Jesus Christ was an invasion, a benevolent takeover whereby everyone and everything in the world would one day be transformed. He announced His purpose at His first coming (John 3:16–17). He has called us to tell others of His free gift of salvation (Acts 1:8), leading them toward the incredible life-transformation that comes with knowing Christ personally (2 Corinthians 5:17).

 Read John 14:1–3.

Where did Jesus say He was going? And why was He going there?

What do you think "the Father's house" is like? Try to describe it with word pictures. What do you think you will see there?

_____

_____

_____

If you are a believer in Christ, how does it make you feel to know that Jesus is preparing a place for you?

_____

_____

OVERCOMING DEATH

On the eve of His trials and execution, Jesus reassured His followers that what He was about to do would change the very nature of death (John 14:19–20; 16:33). No longer would anyone have to fear the permanence of death and decay. For those in His kingdom—those who choose to believe in Him—life after death promised to be a joyous existence (John 15:9–11).

When Jesus promised His disciples "I will come again and receive you to Myself" (John 14:3), He was not speaking of His resurrection but of His coming for them. But because of the oppressive Roman culture they lived in and their traditional Jewish understanding of the Messiah's role, His disciples wondered if Jesus would take the throne of Israel and transform the world into His kingdom (Acts 1:6). Instead, Jesus commissioned His followers to share His message of salvation and heart-transformation until He comes.

Read Acts 1:9–11.

How did Jesus leave the earth?

_____

_____

In what manner will He return? How do you know?

When Jesus ascended into heaven, no one knew how much time would pass before His return (Matthew 24:42). Roughly thirty years afterward, Christians wanted to know what happened to the believers who had died. They asked, "Where are they? What will happen to them when Jesus returns?" We'll take a look at the apostle Paul's answers to their questions. First, however, we must clarify two distinct, yet related issues: death and destiny.

DIFFERENTIATING DEATH AND DESTINY

According to the Bible, death occurs when our immaterial essence—our soul or spirit—is separated from our material body. Death is not the end of life but merely the end of life as we now know it. (For further study, see 1 Corinthians 15:42–57; 2 Corinthians 5:1–10.) While our bodies gradually disintegrate, our souls continue to exist. Where they exist and what happens to them is a matter of destiny.

According to 2 Corinthians 5:8, those who die as believers in Jesus Christ are absent from the body but exist in the presence of the Lord. Those who die as non-believers receive no further opportunity to change their minds. They do not exist in a purgatory until suffering has purged sin from them. Those who die as non-believers face eternal separation from God in a place of torment (2 Thessalonians 1:6–10).

But what will happen to living and dead believers when Christ comes? To answer these questions, Paul revealed a "mystery."

MYSTERIOUSLY TRANSFORMING OUR BODIES

Read 1 Corinthians 15:50–58.
The Greek word translated as "mystery" is *musterion*, which means

"the content of that which has not been known before but which has been revealed."[1] In other words, the Greek idea of a mystery "does not denote an *unknowable* thing, but one which is withdrawn from knowledge or manifestation, and which cannot be known without special manifestation of it."[2] In revealing something to Christians that was previously unknown, Paul first affirmed the fact that our flesh-and-blood bodies cannot last forever (15:50). Even if a person is alive when Christ returns, something must happen to his or her body in order to prepare it for eternal life. Relatively speaking, those who have already died, though their bodies have decayed, are not in any worse condition than those who are alive. When Jesus returns to receive His people to Himself, a radical physical change must—and will—take place.

According to 1 Corinthians 15:51–53, what will happen to believers' bodies at the very first moment of Jesus's return? How much time will this change require?

_____

_____

_____

How will the relationship between believers and death be changed?

_____

_____

So, what will our resurrected bodies be like? Jesus appeared to His disciples after His resurrection, giving a few glimpses of what our physical reality will be. For example, He was visible to His followers with recognizable human attributes (Luke 24:39; John 20:19–20) and He ate with His followers on several occasions (Luke 24:41–43). Like His resurrected body, our new bodies will be perfect, immortal, and imperishable (1 Corinthians 15:54).

DEPARTING FROM THIS EARTH

Paul once again delved into the subject of what kind of future we can expect as Christians in his first letter to the church at Thessalonica. From his words to them, we can learn how to respond to those who "are asleep," meaning those who have died.

 Read 1 Thessalonians 4:13–18.

Paul begins by discussing our grief over believers who have already died. What does he tell us not to do in verse 13? (Be careful to consider the whole verse.) In the next verse, what reason does he give?

_____

_____

_____

Now, consider verses 15–17. When Jesus appears to receive His followers, what three audible signals will announce His arrival?

_____

_____

_____

Who will go to Him first? Then who? And where will they meet Him?

_____

_____

_____

What do you imagine this event will be like? Describe any sights, sounds, emotions, or sensations you expect to experience.

_____

_____

_____

Paul concluded his teaching with the exhortation, "Therefore comfort one another with these words" (1 Thessalonians 4:18). We can endure with hope because Jesus has said, "Do not let your hearts be troubled; believe in God, believe also in Me. . . . I will come again and receive you to Myself, that where I am, there you may be also" (John 14:1, 3).

STARTING YOUR JOURNEY

The Lord will return for us. And now that we understand His plan and purpose for us—both materially and immaterially— one vital question remains. How will we respond in light of what we know?

Paul's words in Titus 2:11–15 prompt us to answer several penetrating questions to this effect. Everyone will be called upon to answer each one of them at some point. So take your time. Read each verse, consider the questions carefully, and then answer honestly.

For the grace of God has appeared, bringing salvation to all men. (Titus 2:11)

Have you received the salvation God has brought to you? How do you know?

_____

_____

_____

_____

_____

If you have not yet begun a relationship with God, you have no reason for hope beyond death on the day Christ returns. You will bear the consequences for your moral failures and be eternally separated from God. But it doesn't have to be this way! If you would like to know more about how to receive the salvation God offers you, read "How to Begin a Relationship with God" at the end of this Bible Companion.

For the grace of God has appeared . . . instructing us to deny ungodliness and worldly desires and to live sensibly, righteously and godly in the present age. (Titus 2:11–12)

Are you living as a true disciple, that is, observing all that Jesus has commanded you?

_____

_____

_____

In what areas do you struggle to deny ungodliness or to live righteously?

_____

_____

_____

Take time to pray, giving these areas to the Lord and asking Him to help you to deal with them in a godly way, growing to become the person He would have you be.

Looking for the blessed hope and the appearing of the glory of our great God and Savior, Christ Jesus. (Titus 2:13)

Are you excited about His appearing? Why, or why not?

_____

_____

_____

Is anything keeping you from being ready? If so, what is it?

_____

_____

_____

[Jesus] gave Himself for us to redeem us from every lawless deed, and to purify for Himself a people for His own possession, zealous for good deeds. (Titus 2:14)

In a practical sense, what does it mean to be "zealous for good deeds"?

_____

_____

_____

Why do you think it is necessary for us to have been "redeemed from lawless deeds" in order to be "zealous for good deeds"?

_____

_____

_____

These things speak and exhort and reprove with all authority. (Titus 2:15)

Summarize verses 11–14 in your own words.

_____

_____

_____

Now briefly describe how we should live while we're waiting for Christ's coming.

_____

_____

_____

As we began our study of Jesus, we considered the question, *Who is this man?* When His accomplishments are viewed through the lens of history, they might not appear very significant. Think of men like Alexander the

Great, Caesar Augustus, and Emperor Constantine, who conquered vast stretches of the known world. Think of Plato, Newton, and Einstein, men who revolutionized the thinking of humankind. Think of all the musicians, composers, philosophers, builders, and leaders who impacted the world positively. Other people have conquered more, written more, and built more. But none have impacted the world more profoundly, permanently, or—for millions of people—more personally than the carpenter from Nazareth.

If all that remains of Jesus are books, songs, and paintings, then He is nothing more than a popular historical figure. Historical figures can impact future generations by virtue of the memories we preserve, but only living persons with whom we have an active relationship can transform us.

Generation after generation of watching, wondering people have wanted to know, *Who is this man?* God preserved a record of His past deeds in the Bible, but He has also provided a living record. Jesus is alive! And the most satisfying answer we can offer to a lost and broken world is the living hope of a living Savior, the proof of which is in the transformed lives of His followers.

Who is this man? He is Jesus, the greatest life of all.

How to Begin a Relationship with God

J esus is the perfect model of a person enjoying intimate fellowship with our heavenly Father and walking closely with Him. However, His example also reveals how imperfect we are. We are separated from God by sin, powerless to restore this relationship on our own. We can never match the example of Jesus. However, we can enjoy intimate fellowship with God through His Son.

If you want to restore your relationship with God, you need to understand four key truths.

OUR SPIRITUAL CONDITION: TOTALLY DEPRAVED

The first truth is rather personal. One look in the mirror of Scripture, and our human condition becomes painfully clear:

There is none righteous, not even one;
There is none who understands,
There is none who seeks for God;
All have turned aside, together they have become useless;
There is none who does good,
There is not even one. (Romans 3:10–12)

We are all sinners through and through—totally depraved. Now, that doesn't mean we've committed every atrocity known to humankind. We're not as *bad* as we can be, just as *bad off* as we can be. Sin colors all our thoughts, motives, words, and actions.

You still don't believe it? Look around. Everything around us bears the smudge marks of our sinful nature. Despite our best efforts to create a perfect world, crime statistics continue to soar, divorce rates keep climbing, and families keep crumbling.

Something has gone terribly wrong in our society and in ourselves; something deadly. Contrary to how the world would repackage it, "me-first" living doesn't equal rugged individuality and freedom; it equals death. As Paul said in his letter the Romans, "The wages of sin is death" (Romans 6:23)—our spiritual and physical death that comes from God's righteous judgment of our sin, along with all of the emotional and practical effects of this separation that we experience on a daily basis. This brings us to the second marker: God's character.

GOD'S CHARACTER: INFINITELY HOLY

How can a good God judge each of us for a sinful state we were born into? Our total depravity is only half the answer. The other half is God's infinite holiness.

The fact that we know things are not as they should be points us to a standard of goodness beyond ourselves. Our sense of injustice in life on this side of eternity implies a perfect standard of justice beyond our reality. That standard and source is God Himself. And God's standard of holiness contrasts starkly with our sinful condition.

Scripture says that "God is Light, and in Him there is no darkness at all" (1 John 1:5). He is absolutely holy—which creates a problem for us. If He is so pure, how can we who are so impure relate to Him?

Perhaps we could try being better people, try to tilt the balance in favor of our good deeds, or seek out methods for self-improvement. Throughout history, people have attempted to live up to God's standard by keeping the Ten Commandments or living by their own code of ethics. Unfortunately, no one can come close to satisfying the demands of God's law. Romans 3:20 says, "For no one can ever be made right in God's sight by doing what his law commands. For the more we know God's law, the clearer it becomes that we aren't obeying it" (NLT).

OUR NEED: A SUBSTITUTE

So here we are, sinners by nature and sinners by choice, trying to pull ourselves up by our own bootstraps to attain a relationship with our holy Creator. But every time we try, we fall flat on our faces. We can't live a good enough life to make up for our sin, because God's standard isn't "good enough"—it's perfection. And we can't make amends for the offense our sin has created without dying for it.

Who can get us out of this mess?

If someone could live perfectly, honoring God's law, and would bear sin's death penalty for us—in our place—then we would be saved from our predicament. But is there such a person? Thankfully, yes!

Meet your substitute—*Jesus Christ*. He is the One who took death's place for you!

[God] made [Jesus Christ] who knew no sin to be sin on our behalf, so that we might become the righteousness of God in Him. (2 Corinthians 5:21)

GOD'S PROVISION: A SAVIOR

God rescued us by sending His Son, Jesus, to die for our sins on the cross (1 John 4:9–10). Jesus was fully human and fully divine (John 1:1, 18), a truth that ensures His understanding of our weaknesses, His power to forgive, and His ability to bridge the gap between God and us (Romans 5:6–11). In short, we are "justified as a gift by His grace through the redemption which is in Christ Jesus" (Romans 3:24). Two words in this verse bear further explanation: *justified* and *redemption.*

Justification is God's act of mercy, in which He declares believing sinners righteous, while they are still in their sinning state. Justification doesn't mean that God *makes* us righteous, so that we never sin again, rather that He *declares* us righteous—much like a judge pardons a guilty criminal. Because Jesus took our sin upon Himself and suffered our judgment on the cross, God forgives our debt and proclaims us PARDONED.

Redemption is God's act of paying the ransom price to release us from our bondage to sin. Held hostage by Satan, we were shackled by the iron chains of sin and death. Like a loving parent whose child has been kidnapped, God willingly paid the ransom for you. And what a price He paid! He gave His only Son to bear our sins—past, present, and future. Jesus's death and resurrection broke our chains and set us free to become children of God (Romans 6:16–18, 22; Galatians 4:4–7).

PLACING YOUR FAITH IN CHRIST

These four truths describe how God has provided a way to Himself through Jesus Christ. Because the price has been paid in full by God, we must respond to His free gift of eternal life in total faith and confidence in Him to save us. We must step forward into the relationship with God that He has prepared for us—not by doing good works or being a good person, but by coming to Him just as we are and accepting His justification and redemption by faith.

> For by grace you have been saved through faith; and that not of yourselves, it is the gift of God; not as a result of works, so that no one should boast. (Ephesians 2:8–9)

We accept God's gift of salvation simply by placing our faith in Christ alone for the forgiveness of our sins. Would you like to enter a relationship with your Creator by trusting in Christ as your Savior? If so, here's a simple prayer you can use to express your faith:

> *Dear God,*
>
> *I know that my sin has put a barrier between You and me. Thank You for sending Your Son, Jesus, to die in my place. I trust in Jesus alone to forgive my sins, and I accept His gift of eternal life. I ask Jesus to be my personal Savior and the Lord of my life. Thank You. In Jesus's name, amen.*

If you've prayed this prayer or one like it and you wish to find out more about knowing God and His plan for you in the Bible, contact us at Insight for Living. You can speak to one of our pastors on staff by calling 972-473-5097, e-mail us at www.insight.org/contactapastor, or write to us at the address below.

No other decision can compare with the one that puts you in a right relationship with God through His Son, Jesus Christ, who loved us and gave Himself for us.

Pastoral Ministries Department
Insight for Living
Post Office Box 269000
Plano, Texas 75026-9000

Clearing Away the Clutter of Unresolved Sin

Once you have placed your trust in Jesus Christ to save you from the penalty of your sins, you never again have to worry about condemnation—not from other people and not even from God (Romans 8:1). Guilt and shame have no place in the life of a believer; however, we are still prone to sin. We will fail in our efforts to live a life that honors God, and we will inevitably harm others by the poor choices we make and the sinful acts we commit. However, because Jesus paid the penalty for our sin, we will never suffer the eternal consequences for our wrongdoing. However, unresolved sins can nonetheless complicate our lives with earthly consequences, frustrate the Lord's desire to bless us, and cause others great heartache. Despite our secure relationship with God, sin is still a deadly serious matter.

Fortunately, the Lord has given us a means by which we can clear away the clutter of wrongdoing. If you have unresolved sin in your life, consider taking the following steps, which give practical application to principles taught in Scripture (Matthew 18:15–17; Romans 12:17–21; Ephesians 4:25–27; 1 John 1:9).

Stop. Accept the truth of your poor choices or outright sin and own the responsibility for the damage your action or inaction has caused.

Confess. Confess your failure to the Lord in prayer and commit yourself to turning from it. Ask Him for His help. He has promised to provide you with the strength to meet this challenge (1 Corinthians 10:13). If your sin has harmed another person, go to him or her and admit how you have failed or have contributed to making a situation worse. Be careful not to include any mention of his or her wrongdoing (even if it is greater than your own), and resist the temptation to minimize yours.

Restore. Apologize, showing genuine concern for how you have hurt the other person and damaged your relationship. Your sorrow should reflect the level of his or her pain.

Rest. Receive the Lord's forgiveness and accept that the other person may or may not respond as you might desire. Forgiveness is not something you deserve or have the right to demand. His or her choice to forgive must be made freely.

Review. Without being too hard on yourself, try to discover *why* you chose to act as you did. Choices arise from expectations—usually unconscious ones. Ask the Lord to show you what you don't see so that you can replace destructive coping with constructive choosing (Psalm 139:23–24). Then ask Him to cleanse you heart of any desire for sin (Psalm 51:10).

This is not a magic formula. It is not something you must do to please God or to earn His favor. Because Christ died for your sins and rose from the dead to give you life, your heavenly Father will always be pleased with you. These steps are merely a means by which you can keep your life free from the distractions and hindrances of unresolved sin. The Lord has blessings in store that exceed your wildest imaginings. Don't let anything come between you!

Notes

Unless otherwise noted below, all material in this Bible Companion is adapted from "Jesus: The Greatest Life of All" a sermon series and companion book by Charles R. Swindoll and was supplemented by the Creative Ministries department of Insight for Living.

Lesson One

1. C. S. Lewis, *Mere Christianity*, rev. and enl. ed. (New York: The Macmillan Company, 1958), 40. Copyright © C. S. Lewis Pte. Ltd. 1942, 1943, 1944, 1952. Extract reprinted by permission.

2. Ray Stedman, *Adventuring through the Bible: A Comprehensive Guide to the Entire Bible* (Grand Rapids: Discovery House Publishers, 1997), 528. Copyright © 1997 by Elaine Stedman. Used by permission of Discovery House Publishers, Box 3566, Grand Rapids, MI 49501. All rights reserved.

3. Lewis, *Mere Christianity*, 40–41.

Lesson Two

1. Gerhard Kittel and Gerhard Friedrich, eds., *Theological Dictionary of the New Testament*, abridged ed. in one volume, ed. and trans. Geoffrey W. Bromiley (Grand Rapids: William B. Eerdmans, 1967), 786.

2. Gerhard Kittel and Gerhard Friedrich, eds., *Theological Dictionary of the New Testament*, abridged ed. in one volume, ed. and trans. Geoffrey W. Bromiley (Grand Rapids: William B. Eerdmans, 1967), 828.

3. W. Phillip Keller, *Rabboni . . . Which Is to Say Master* (Old Tappan, N.J.: Fleming H. Revell Company, 1977), 68.

4. *Merriam-Webster's Collegiate Dictionary*, 10th ed, see "impassible."

5. J. Daane, "Unchangeability of God," in *The International Standard Bible Encyclopedia*, vol. 4, Q–Z, rev. ed., ed. Geoffrey W. Bromiley and others (Grand Rapids: Wm. B. Eerdmans, 1988), 943.

Lesson Three

1. Jane Polley, ed., *American Folklore and Legend* (Pleasantville, NY: Reader's Digest Association, Inc., 1979), 393.

2. Charles Colson and Ellen Santilli Vaughn, *Kingdoms in Conflict* (n.p., William Morrow/Zondervan Publishing House, 1987), 81.

3. R. Earle, "Inn," in *The International Standard Bible Encyclopedia*, vol. 2, E–J, rev. ed., ed. Geoffrey W. Bromiley and others (Grand Rapids: Wm. B. Eerdmans, 1988), 826.

4. Gerhard Kittel and Gerhard Friedrich, eds., *Theological Dictionary of the New Testament*, abridged ed. in one volume, ed. and trans. Geoffrey W. Bromiley (Grand Rapids: William B. Eerdmans, 1967), 426.

5. Thomas Mott Osborne, *Within Prison Walls* (New York: D. Appleton and Company, 1914), 24.

6. Craig S. Keener, *The IVP Bible Background Commentary: New Testament* (Downers Grove, Ill.: InterVarsity Press, 1993), 194.

Notes

Lesson Four

1. Gerhard Kittel and Gerhard Friedrich, eds., *Theological Dictionary of the New Testament*, abridged ed. in one volume, ed. and trans. Geoffrey W. Bromiley (Grand Rapids: William B. Eerdmans, 1967), 1174–5.

2. H.G. Liddell. *A Lexicon: Abridged from Liddell and Scott's Greek-English Lexicon* (Oak Harbor, Wash.: Logos Research Systems, Inc., 1996), electronic ed.

3. *Nelson's Illustrated Bible Dictionary*, ed. Herbert Lockyer, Sr. (Nashville: Thomas Nelson Publishers, 1986), see "wise men," 1104.

4. M.G. Easton. *Easton's Bible Dictionary* (Oak Harbor, Wash.: Logos Research Systems, Inc., 1996), electronic ed.

Lesson Five

1. Benjamin Franklin, available at http://usinfo.state.gov/scv/Archive/2006/Jan/06-875137.html, accessed February 12, 2007.

2. R. Laird Harris, Gleason Leonard Archer and Bruce K. Waltke, *Theological Wordbook of the Old Testament*, vol. 2 (Chicago: Moody Press, 1980), 1030.

3. Harris and others, *Theological Wordbook of the Old Testament*, 420.

4. Gerhard Kittel and Gerhard Friedrich, eds., *Theological Dictionary of the New Testament*, abridged ed. in one volume, ed. and trans. Geoffrey W. Bromiley (Grand Rapids: William B. Eerdmans, 1967), 829.

5. Irenaeus, "Against Heresies," *The Writings of Irenaeus*, trans. Alexander Roberts and W.H. Rambaut, vol. 1 (Edinburgh: T&T Clark, 1874), 444.

6. Jim Elliot, *The Journals of Jim Elliot*, ed. Elisabeth Elliot (Grand Rapids: Fleming H. Revell, 2003), 174 (journal entry from October 28, 1949).

Lesson Six

1. See "Top 200 Prescription Drugs of 2005," *Pharmacy Times*, May 2006, www.pharmacytimes.com/article.cfm?ID=3468, accessed January 18, 2007..

2. Marvin R. Vincent, *Word Studies in the New Testament*, vol. 1 (New York: Charles Scribner's Sons, 1900), 67.

3. Gerhard Kittel, ed., *Theological Dictionary of the New Testament*, vol. 3, ed. and trans. Geoffrey W. Bromiley (Grand Rapids: William B. Eerdmans, 1972), 827.

4. Gerhard Kittel and Gerhard Friedrich, eds., *Theological Dictionary of the New Testament*, abridged ed. in one volume, ed. and trans. Geoffrey W. Bromiley (Grand Rapids: William B. Eerdmans, 1967), 1252.

5. Gerhard Kittel and Gerhard Friedrich, eds., *Theological Dictionary of the New Testament*, abridged ed. in one volume, ed. and trans. Geoffrey W. Bromiley (Grand Rapids: William B. Eerdmans, 1967), 56.

6. William Hendriksen, *New Testament Commentary: Exposition of the Gospel According to Matthew* (Grand Rapids: Baker Book House, 1982), 504.

7. Gerhard Friedrich, ed., *Theological Dictionary of the New Testament*, vol. 9, ed. and trans. Geoffrey W. Bromiley (Grand Rapids: William B. Eerdmans, 1974), 483.

Lesson Seven

1. Robert L. Wise, *Your Churning Place: Your Emotions—Turning Stress into Strength* (Glendale, Calif.: Regal Books, 1977), 9–10.

2. Kenneth S. Wuest, *Wuest's Word Studies from the Greek New Testament: For the English Reader*, vol. 2 (Grand Rapids: Eerdmans, 1975).

Notes

Lesson Eight

1. Robert L. Thomas, *Revelation 8–22: An Exegetical Commentary* (Chicago: Moody Press, 1995), 433..

2. Thomas, *Revelation 8–22: An Exegetical Commentary*, 440.

3. G. K. Beale, *The Book of Revelation: A Commentary on the Greek Text* (Grand Rapids: Wm. B. Eerdmans, 1999), 1042.

4. Thomas, *Revelation 8–22: An Exegetical Commentary*, 440.

5. Charles R. Swindoll, *Parenting: From Surviving to Thriving* (Nashville: Word Publishing Group, 2006), 239–240.

Lesson Nine

1. John F. Walvoord and Roy B. Zuck, eds. *The Bible Knowledge Commentary: New Testament* (Colorado Springs: Victor Books, 1989), 834.

Lesson Ten

1. *Merriam-Webster's Collegiate Dictionary*, 10ᵗʰ ed., "abide."

2. Gerhard Kittel, ed., *Theological Dictionary of the New Testament*, vol. 1, ed. and trans. Geoffrey W. Bromiley (Grand Rapids: Wm. B. Eerdmans, 1964), 185.

3. Kittel, ed., *Theological Dictionary of the New Testament*, 185.

4. Warren W. Wiersbe, *The Bible Exposition Commentary*, vol. 1 (Wheaton, Ill.: Victor Books, 1994), 356–7.

5. Author unknown.

Lesson Eleven

1. Alfred Edersheim, *The Life and Times of Jesus the Messiah*, vol. 2 (Grand Rapids: William B. Eerdmans, 1962), 11.

2. James Swanson, *Dictionary of Biblical Languages with Semantic Domains: Hebrew* (Oak Harbor, Wash.,: Logos Research Systems, Inc., 1997), electronic ed.

Lesson Twelve

1. William Barclay, *The Master's Men* (New York: Abingdon Press, 1959), 74.

2. Robert L. Thomas and W. Don Wilkins, eds. *Exhaustive Concordance of the Bible: Hebrew–Aramaic and Greek Dictionaries*, updated ed. (Anaheim, Calif.: Foundation Publications, 1998), 1540.

3. Marvin R.Vincent, *Word Studies in the New Testament*, vol. 1 (New York: Charles Scribner's Sons, 1903), 141.

Lesson Thirteen

1. "Cohort," *Encyclopedia Britannica*, 2007, www.britannica.com/eb/article-9022105, accessed August 5, 2007.

2. Bromiley, Geoffrey W., eds., *International Standard Bible Encyclopedia*, rev. ed., vol. 1, (Grand Rapids: William B. Eerdmans, 1988), 128.

3. Bromiley, Geoffrey W., eds., *International Standard Bible Encyclopedia*, 128.

Lesson Fourteen

1. "The Apostles' Creed," *Trinity Hymnal*, rev.ed. (Atlanta: Great Commission, 1990), 845.

2. Marvin R. Vincent, *Word Studies in the New Testament*, vol. 2 (New York: Charles Scribner's Sons, 1903), 277.

Notes

Lesson Fifteen

1. Cicero, as quoted in Frederick T. Zugibe, *The Crucifixion of Jesus: A Forensic Inquiry* (New York: M. Evans and Company, Inc., 2005), 51. Used by permission of Rowman & Littlefield Publishing Group.

2. Zugibe, *The Crucifixion of Jesus*, 51.

3. Zugibe, *The Crucifixion of Jesus*, 53.

4. Zugibe, *The Crucifixion of Jesus*, 22.

5. Zugibe, *The Crucifixion of Jesus*, 92.

6. Zugibe, *The Crucifixion of Jesus*, 92.

7. W.D. Edwards, W.J. Gabel, and F.E. Hosmer, "On the Physical Death of Jesus Christ," *The Journal of the American Medical Association*, 255, no. 11 (March 21, 1986): 1461.

8. Edwards, Gabel, and Hosmer, On the Physical Death of Jesus Christ," 1461.

Lesson Sixteen

1. W. H. Mare, "Burial," Merrill C. Tenney, gen. ed., *The Zondervan Pictorial Encyclopedia of the Bible*, vol. 1, A–C, (Grand Rapids: Zondervan, 1975), 673–4.

2. Merrill C. Tenney, *The Reality of the Resurrection* (New York: Harper & Row, Publishers, 1963), 119. Used by permission of HarperCollins Publishers.

Lesson Seventeen

1. Walter Bauer, William F. Arndt, and F. Wilbur Gingrich, *A Greek-English Lexicon of the New Testament and Other Early Christian Literature* (Chicago: The University of Chicago Press, 1979), 565.

2. Walter Bauer, William F. Arndt, and F. Wilbur Gingrich, *A Greek-English Lexicon of the New Testament and Other Early Christian Literature*, 775.

3. For a sample survey of the Old Testament, read Genesis 3:15; Numbers 21:6–9; Deuteronomy 18:15–18; Psalms 16:9–11; 22; 69; Isaiah 9, 11, 52:14–53:12; Jeremiah 23:5–6; Zechariah 12:10; 13:7; Daniel 9:26.

4. Robert L. Thomas, *New American Standard Hebrew-Aramaic and Greek Dictionaries: Updated Edition* (Anaheim: Foundation Publications, Inc., 1998, 1981), electronic edition. Accessed through Libronix. See "dianoigo."

5. Louw, Johannes P., and Eugene Albert Nida. Greek-English Lexicon of the New Testament: Based on Semantic Domains, electronic ed. of the 2nd edition (New York: United Bible Societes, 1996). Accessed through Libronix. See "epiginosko."

6. Walter Bauer, William F. Arndt, and F. Wilbur Gingrich, *A Greek-English Lexicon of the New Testament and Other Early Christian Literature*, 124.

Lesson Eighteen

1. Gerhard Kittel, ed., *Theological Dictionary of the New Testament*, Abridged in One Volume (Grand Rapids: William B. Eerdmans Publishing Co., 1985), 1262.

2. Gerhard Kittel, ed., *Theological Dictionary of the New Testament*, Abridged in One Volume (Grand Rapids: William B. Eerdmans Publishing Co., 1985), 7.

Lesson Nineteen

1. Walter Bauer, William F. Arndt, and F. Wilbur Gingrich, *A Greek-English Lexicon of the New Testament and Other Early Christian Literature* (Chicago: The University of Chicago Press, 1979), 692.

2. Daniel B. Wallace, *Greek Grammar Beyond the Basics: Exegetical Syntax of the New Testament* (Grand Rapids: Zondervan Publishing House, 1999), 645.

Notes

Lesson Twenty

1. Johannes P. Louw and Eugene Albert Nida, *Greek-English Lexicon of the New Testament: Based on Semantic Domains*, 2nd edition., vol. 1 (New York: United Bible societies, 1989), 344.

2. Marvin Richardson Vincent, *Word Studies in the New Testament*, vol. 1 (Bellingham, WA: Logos Research Systems, Inc., 2002), Note on Matthew 13:11.

Resources for Probing Further

The apostle John, who lived three years with Jesus, closed his gospel by saying, "There are so many other things Jesus did. If they were all written down, each of them, one by one, I can't imagine a world big enough to hold such a library of books" (John 21:25 MSG).

Well, a global-sized library of books about Jesus obviously hasn't been written, but there are many helpful books to choose from. So, if you'd like to further your study of the life and work of Jesus Christ, we recommend the following works written or edited by Bible-believing scholars. Of course, we cannot always endorse everything a writer or ministry says, so we encourage you to approach these and all other non-biblical resources with wisdom and discernment.

For Personal Study

Lucado, Max. *He Chose the Nails*. Nashville: Thomas Nelson Publishers, 2005.

Lucado, Max. *Six Hours One Friday: Living in the Power of the Cross*. Nashville: Thomas Nelson, 2005.

Pentecost, J. Dwight. *A Harmony of the Words and Works of Jesus Christ*. Grand Rapids: Zondervan Publishing House, 1981.

Pentecost, J. Dwight. *The Words and Works of Jesus Christ: A Study of the Life of Christ*. Grand Rapids: Zondervan Publishing House, 2000.

Stott, John R. W. *The Cross of Christ*. Downers Grove: InterVarsity Press, 2006.

Swindoll, Charles R. *A Bethlehem Christmas: Celebrating the Joyful Season*. Nashville: Thomas Nelson Publishers, 2007.

Witmer, John A. *Immanuel: Experiencing Jesus as Man and God*. Nashville: Word Publishing, 1998.

For Advanced Learning

Bock, Darrell L. *Studying the Historical Jesus: A Guide to Sources and Methods.* Grand Rapids: Baker Academic, 2002.

Hoehner, Harold W. *Chronological Aspects of the Life of Christ.* Grand Rapids: Zondervan Publishing House, 1978.